Make Your Internship Count

Make Your Internship Count

Find, Launch, and Embrace Your Career

Marti Fischer

Leader in applied, concise business books

First published in 2023 by
Business Expert Press, LLC
222 East 46th Street, New York, NY 10017
www.businessexpertpress.com

ISBN-13: 978-1-63742-557-2 (paperback)
ISBN-13: 978-1-63742-558-9 (e-book)

Business Expert Press Business Career Development Collection

First edition: 2023

10 9 8 7 6 5 4 3 2 1

For Jack and Kat
Who once were interns and are now fully employed

Description

Moving from student to employee can be a scary transition. *Make Your Internship Count* takes you step by step, from the initial decision to pursue an internship through pitching a full-time job, to make your leap into the working world easier and less stressful.

This book gives you a competitive advantage and tells you what employers expect, including how to meet those expectations. *Make Your Internship Count's* easy-to-read format offers prompts, exercises, worksheets, and "This Really Happened" stories to:

- ✓ Find internship opportunities that fit your skills and interests.
- ✓ Set and deliver on an internship goal.
- ✓ Interview with style.
- ✓ Make a great first impression.
- ✓ Navigating remote and hybrid internships.
- ✓ Speak comfortably about compensation.
- ✓ Communicate effectively with peers and bosses.
- ✓ Accept criticism and feedback the right way.
- ✓ Create a memorable last impression.
- ✓ Build a lasting professional network.

With input from HR pros, executives, and former interns, *Make Your Internship Count* gives you what you need to *find your path and launch your career.*

Keywords

internship advice; first job advice; finding your career path; skills employers want; navigating the business world; insider interview tips; building a professional network

Contents

Testimonials

"Marti is awesome! She helped me get into the professional world and I would have been a lot more confused without her."—**Charlie Bohnsack, rising college senior**

"Marti has written an engaging, practical book that will serve students and employers alike! She provides concrete suggestions and real-world examples that are valuable beyond the internship program. I heartily recommend it!" —**Julie Baker, COO and cofounder, Ursa Space Systems**

"Our son graduated college with dual degrees and a minor in his chosen field. He just didn't know how to make a job in his field happen. As parents, we recognize that entering the work world today vastly differs from our experience. Finding a job and embarking on a desired career that aligns with your values and strengths is a skill that isn't taught at college. Marti's in-the-know expertise, support and effective engagement brought him from a motivated yet unsure college grad to an independent, launched young man thriving in an industry of his choice."—**Nancy Gany, parent**

"Every successful startup CEO I know had an early internship experience that helped set them on the path to leadership. Marti's book details how to set yourself on that path."—**Brad Treat, Instructor, Entrepreneurship, SC Johnson College of Business, Cornell University**

"This is essential reading for young people looking to find their way in the business world, for people like myself who interview and hire young people, and department heads who lead internship programs. But I think I love this book most as a parent with young adult children entering the job force. This is full of great advice written with clarity, without ridiculous business jargon and with the insight of real-world experience that can be received and digested so much better than if it came from a parent."—**Adam Isidore, Creative Production Executive/Consultant**

"I was one of the first eyes to read Make Your Internship Count: Find, Launch, and Embrace Your Career—*truly a must-have for any upcoming college student. It is a guide for those looking to 'break into' the world of internships and truly conquer an internship each step of the way. Marti delivers a phenomenal, easy-to-follow roadmap that is current as the workplace has evolved since the pandemic. It's a resource for young professionals and a must-have for any parent or professional with an intern or two roaming their hallways. This will be a definite resource for me on my HR mantle!"*—**Mohamed Ali, Global Senior Vice President, Human Resources, Dow Jones**

"This book is a must-read for anyone navigating the Internship process. It's full of practical tips and put together in an easy-to-navigate format." —**Gina LaRussa, SVP, Human Resources, NBCUniversal**

"Marti's book is like a cheat code for anyone wanting to make the most of their internship. This step-by-step guide empowers you to approach every aspect of your internship—even the less comfortable aspects, like constructive feedback and compensation discussions—and prepares you to crush it in your next career phase."—**Josh Riman, Founder and President, Great Believer**

"This is a book that anyone finding their career path should read. Marti's easy-to-read, step-by-step format effectively builds your skills and gets a leg up on your competition."—**Chris Pizzurro, Principal, Leap Media Group LLC**

"Internships are an important part of companies developing new talent. I always believed that if an intern candidate came in prepared and curious that they would be worth our time to teach and mentor. In many cases, we hired those candidates full-time after their internship. Marti's book will supply you with a clear roadmap to prepare for the interview and give you the important tools to make your internship as successful as possible." —**Harry Keeshan, President (Retired), PHD Media**

Preface

A Note From Marti

Why You Need This Book—or Not

You've picked up this book either because you like the cover or because you're a year or two away from college graduation, thinking, "Everyone is telling me I should get an internship before I graduate."

It's a bold move to give up 6 to 10 weeks of summer fun to explore the working world. But it's a good idea.

Whether you're thinking about career options, making some money for yourself, or looking to get an edge on the competition for jobs, an internship is a strong first step. This book will help you navigate the process of identifying how you can provide value to your prospective employers, finding those opportunities, and making sure you get the most out of them.

More importantly, *Make Your Internship Count* will guide you through the single biggest transition in your life so far: *the transition from student to professional*. It will get you talking about yourself the *right* way and asking the *right* questions and help you find the *right internship for you*. After all, you deserve to meet inspiring people, make money, and have fun doing it—if you put in a little work.

The Beauty of "Owning" Your Internship Hunt

Your career is just that—*yours*. Unlike the town you grew up in or the classes you took for a degree, there are no hard-and-fast requirements written out anywhere. Some people find this lack of restrictions to be incredibly liberating; others can find themselves easily paralyzed by the lack of guidelines or guardrails.

Whichever camp you fall into, make no mistake: You get to own every step of your career. Students seeking internships or postgraduation jobs point out that this level of ownership is what makes starting a career intimidating, especially when other people around you think they have a "right" place for you to start. Regardless of what they think or what you choose, you get to own it. You, and only you, get to experience every major win and tough review session, company holiday, and late-night grind.

The beauty of an internship is that you get to learn about what you like and don't like—about a type of managerial style, company culture, and the work itself. Not every job is glamorous (especially internships and entry-level jobs), but if it sets you on the path to doing something you love, you're that much closer to pursuing it after graduation. If you don't love it, then there's no harm and no foul (but there are still many ways to leverage it to help you get where you want to go, which we will discuss in later chapters).

The most important thing at the end of the day is that you're happy with what you do. Perhaps the most important thing an internship can tell you is "Will I be happy here?" and help explain "why?" or "why not?" With that knowledge, you're not just better equipped to talk with your parents at dinner or answer interview questions—you're setting yourself up to wake up and be genuinely happy in your postgraduation life.

Make Your Internship Count will help you sell your strengths, defend your weaknesses, and determine if you are a "good fit" for a company. It offers advice and direction for just about everything you will encounter during your internship, helping you perform well without causing unnecessary stress.

Still, if you're not sure about buying this book, or if you're unsure that an internship is worth your time and energy, take a few minutes and read the next five pages. They spell out exactly what you'll get from your purchase.

Let's start at the end.

A successful internship gives you *a key advantage in landing a full-time job, in many cases, even before you graduate.* And with a full-time job, you can begin your life as an independent person.

Now, I don't want to make this sound too easy. You'll have competition. When you toss your cap in the air, there will be about four million other unemployed folks doing the same thing. It's a group that includes:

- 2.0 million newly minted bachelor's degree recipients
- 1.0 million associate degree holders
- 1.0 million new advanced degree recipients

Source: U.S. Department of Education, National Center for Education Statistics, 2019 to 2020.

Companies are working harder than ever to find employees worth keeping and keeping their current employees happy. That search begins with finding interns—it's a trial run for both of you! *Make Your Internship Count* will prepare you with a plan, a timeline, activities to help you succinctly explain who you are, and prepare you with great responses for the "make-or-break" situations you'll face along the way.

Why an Internship Is a Good Idea

Getting into the *right* internship program involves a bit of work on your part. Is it worth it? Consider this:

- **70 percent of new hires by large companies are from the intern pool.** (Think Facebook, Google, Enterprise Rent-a-Car, Goldman Sachs, etc.)
- **In some industries, internships are the largest percentage of entry-level job postings.** (Think digital, IT, graphic design, engineering, marketing, etc.)
- **Students who accept a job after their junior year internship won't have to look for a job during senior year!**

Source: J. Selingo. 2016. *There Is Life After College.* New York, NY: Harper Collins.

As an intern, you'll get to develop and apply your strongest skills and learn new skills *in real time against real business challenges!* And then you'll be able to add *that* experience to the story of you as a professional.

Your internship experience, well told, is what companies look for when hiring and promoting full-time employees.

Why Companies Hire Interns

Companies hire interns for two reasons.

First, interns bring new thinking to business challenges. After all, *you* and your friends are likely to make up that company's next generation of customers. Companies really do want to know what you think.

Second, internships allow a company to "test drive" potential employees without an expensive and lengthy onboarding process. Interns don't receive benefits such as access to profit sharing or 401K plans. But if the "fit" is right, there's often an opportunity to talk about *future employment*. Win–win!

But don't expect that your 4.0 GPA or that you were the captain of a varsity team or president of every club on campus is a slam dunk for getting an internship. To people in the business world, these are just interesting facts—basic resume stuff. These experiences may get you an interview. Once you're hired, employers want to see you confidently apply the skills you've developed from your past experiences against real business challenges. And if you don't have a 4.0 GPA, it's all the more reason for you to craft a creative, applicable narrative to help you get your foot in the door.

This is what employers are looking and listening for:

- Stories or experiences that demonstrate that you've researched the company
- Insight into how you think about challenges
- *Why* the company should hire you
- *How* you think you'll contribute
- Talking and writing about yourself in clear, concise, business-appropriate language

Simply put, employers want to hear what's on your mind, not only about what's on your resume.

Step by step, *Make Your Internship Count* is a guide for developing, delivering, and living up to your *personal business narrative*. If you don't know what a personal business narrative is, don't worry, it's covered in the book.

Who Should Read This Book

Make Your Internship Count **is about *telling your story, delivering on your promises, and making you a valuable addition* to the company where you intern**.

This book is written to help two groups of people. I call them the "Automatics" and the "Nonautomatics."

An Automatic has personal business connections who will make introductions. That friend or family member will get you started with an interview *somewhere* and provide insight into how a company or industry works. This book will make sure the "somewhere" is the "rightwhere." This book will also make sure that, if you are an Automatic, you live up to the expectations that often go along with personal connections.

If you're a "Nonautomatic," someone that wants to break into a business but has no personal connections to leverage, *Make Your Internship Count* will give you the path for leveling the playing field with the Automatics and achieving your goal—quickly.

And for both groups, after you land the *right* internship, *Make Your Internship Count* will help you succeed once you get there.

The advice in this book is laid out to help you handle yourself well during every stage of your internship, from your first networking conversation to your last day on the job. And then we'll talk about how to adapt your narrative to *launch your career*.

Acknowledgments

This book would not have happened without tireless input and advice from employers, HR directors, college internship directors, parents, and students. They know who they are, but if I mention them by name, they'll be flooded with applications and networking requests. The employers represent Fortune 500 companies, media companies, and highly competitive colleges. All have extensive experience in hiring and training interns, and I am grateful for their support and the opportunity to mine their experiences. I would also like to thank several cohorts of the Ithaca College ICNYC Internship Program. They asked great questions about employers, working with colleagues, and general business practices and had amazing stories to tell. There were a lot of laughs in hearing my children's friends' experiences and stories.

Without the combined decades of experience of Mo Ali, Candy Channing, Mark Harrad, and Brad Treat, this book would not have been published. They agreed to read drafts on planes and on vacation and gave honest and diverse feedback. If this book is helpful for you, it's because of them. If you like the title, thank Rick Snyder and Barry Fischer—it's the product of their great collaboration. If you relate to the artwork, it's the result of Carole Bolger's artistic skills.

I would also like to thank Shelly Palmer for his advice about publishing and Ellen Lohman for her eagle-eye proofreading skills.

Saving the best for last is a huge and grateful "thank you" to my husband, an epic editor and my unflagging champion, and my children and their significant others who read drafts, edited fiercely, and brought the millennial point of view.

Introduction

Make Your Internship Count sets you up for the entire intern experience—from the moment you decide to pursue an internship to your last day and final goodbye. Then, you can take everything you've learned with you as you begin your career.

How *Make Your Internship Count* Is Organized

Part 1: Finding Your Path

Part 1 focuses on the prep work that takes you from the idea of pursuing merely an internship to actually accepting a position.

What's included: Setting smart, achievable goals; figuring out your skills; putting together a resume that doesn't put people to sleep; and developing a narrative that makes your network want to help. It's also about *nailing* the interview—by asking the right questions, talking comfortably about compensation, and using the right words for accepting or declining an offer.

Part 2: You're In!

Part 2 prepares you for real-life situations you may encounter during your internship.

What's included: From how to create a great first impression to exceeding employer expectations and how to act in the elevator, to techniques for forming lasting relationships with the other interns and staff. We will also cover how to personally excel *and* be humble while working collaboratively.

Part 3: Launching Your Career

Part 3 is about managing yourself and your surroundings well, especially through the inevitable times of uncertainty or conflict.

What's included: How to communicate effectively with your supervisors, staff, and intern squad and manage yourself in new situations. Part 3 will help you develop the proactive and solutions-oriented mindset that will make you valuable and successful throughout your career. Finally, it will set you up to make a great last impression and leave your internship well.

What You'll Find in Each Chapter

- An **opening summary**, so you'll know what to expect
- **Activities** that make the process real
- Easy-to-eyeball **What to Do/Not Do** lists
- Tips for **building the tools** you need to succeed
- A **Down and Dirty Recap** that sums up the chapter
- **What I Know Now**—a place for your thoughts and ideas

And throughout, you'll read **This Really Happened** stories about every aspect of the internship process. These are true stories that happened to people just like you.

So, if you're ready to *make your internship count*, turn the page. Your journey awaits!

PART 1

Finding Your Path

CHAPTER 1

Choosing Your Direction

What You'll Get From This Chapter

Everything you need to know to develop your personal business narrative and get an internship is already in your head. I promise. With little bit of work and honest thinking from you, this chapter will draw it out. Chapter 1 is dedicated to exploration. In this chapter, we'll define what you like, don't like, what you're good at, and how you work best. With this information, you'll begin to develop your narrative for talking about your value to potential employers.

So before you start updating or writing a resume or scheduling interviews, let's first *figure out the types of places you want to apply*. To move you toward the right organizations and opportunities, let's figure out what you want and don't want in an internship. Let's start with some basics:

- Understanding the connections that exist between your academic life and your social life
- Identifying what you think you'd like to do
- Recognizing how you work best

For example, do you see yourself venturing down the corporate road or into a start-up?

Perhaps you're attracted to a business that simply sounds interesting.

Or maybe you're attracted to an opportunity where you'll spend six weeks in a different part of the country.

We will answer these questions here so you can move toward the experience *you* want later. By the end of this chapter, you'll be working on your personal business narrative.

Activity: *Define Yourself*

This is an exercise to figure out how you work best based on what you like to do, how you interact at school or at a current job, or what you liked about a past job. You'll also figure out what you don't like.

Discovering what you *don't* want to do and where you *don't* want to work is valuable learning. It will weed out internships that won't be fulfilling.

When you can combine who you are with what you like to do, you've already taken the first step toward finding a great internship experience.

Let's begin with a few prompts:

- Do you prefer to work alone or as part of a team?
- How do you best communicate with others? Text, e-mail, phone, video chat, in person?
- Do you have a preference for specific types of working environments? (Check all that apply.)
  - Highly structured
  - Loose and laid back
  - Team-oriented
  - Independent or remote worker-driven
- When you are working on a school project or at a part-time job, what comes easiest for you? These are your strengths.
- Under the same circumstances, what is hardest for you? These are your weaknesses.

Keep these answers handy. A more in-depth activity follows.

Digging Deeper

Now, let's look for the common themes between your academics and your free time, because knowing these common elements define how you prefer to work and makes it easier to figure out the kind of internship that will work best for you. In this section, we'll:

- Lay out the ways in which you work best.
- Understand what attracts you to your free-time activities and academic focus.
- Figure out how you like to work and engage with others.

With this activity, you'll have the beginning of a *great* answer for Human Resources (HR) or the People team when they ask, "Why are you interested in an internship here?"

When you are working through the questions, write down your answers. Then you'll have notes for the networking conversations and interviews to come, and you will be prepared for the make-or-break interview questions, like "Tell me something relevant about you that's not in your resume!" Because that moment, handled well, can lead to a productive conversation about your work habits and how you'll fit within the culture of the organization. And if that conversation goes well, you will be one big step closer to landing an internship.

Now, let's get a little more detailed.

How I Like to Work: Academics and Hobbies

List the areas that you are interested in pursuing. You can list multiple areas. If you are not sure or are "undeclared," make your best guess.

What I Love About My Major

Consider all aspects—the material, the class work, the types of assigned homework, the work you present in class, as well as why you chose it in the first place. Do you have a vision for what you want to do one day that your major sets you up for? List the key people involved in your area of study and what you like about them.

What I Hate About My Major

Consider all aspects—the material, the class work, the types of homework assigned, and the work you present in class. Is there part of what you're studying that you never, ever want to pursue professionally? List the key people involved in your area of study and what you don't like about them.

How I Like to Work

Alone or in a group? Early in the day or late at night? In the library or in your dorm room?

How I Get My Ideas Across to Others

Are you most persuasive verbally, visually, in writing, or some combination? Add supporting examples. The examples become the stories you can draw on during your networking meetings and interviews.

How I Spend My Free Time

What do you do? Are you in groups, in pairs, or alone? Do you work out or hang out? Play beer pong, video games, or strategy games? Draw, play a sport, or some combination?

What I Love About My Friends

What personality traits do you love in your friends? This becomes important when you're asking questions about company culture. You'll want a culture that feels familiar and one in which you believe you can contribute.

My Hobbies

What are your favorite hobbies? What do they do for you? Are they:

- An escape from the academic workload?
- A creative outlet?
- A counterbalance to your academics?

If so, in what way?

(Chances are that you do some combination of things.)

Similarities Between My Major and My Hobbies

What are the behaviors common to both areas? For example, if you enjoy studying alone in a quiet space, writing papers, hanging out with one or two friends, and playing video games, the common ground or shared characteristic lies in *one-on-one activities* and controlled environments.

Alternatively, if you enjoy group projects, presenting in front of the class, playing club sports, and epic fraternity parties, you may enjoy *fast-paced environments* and thrive on *unpredictable days*.

Remember, there are no wrong answers!

Payoff: Conclusions That Become Part of Your Personal Business Narrative

Draw conclusions about the habits you prefer and the conditions under which you are most productive. Be honest with yourself here!

Your answers are the foundation of your personal business narrative and will direct you toward, and away from, certain working environments.

For example, someone who studies alone, enjoys writing papers over making presentations, and plays video games may enjoy an internship in a smaller firm that has a research and analysis component.

Alternatively, if you enjoy group projects, public speaking, club sports, and fraternity parties, you may want to consider opportunities in large, multidepartment, externally facing organizations, like sales departments.

What If You're Somewhere in the Middle?

What if you enjoy writing papers, playing video games with friends, and going to parties? Think about when you are happiest and the activities you're pursuing at that time. Then define the environment where you work best and are most comfortable. That is probably where you will do your best work and have the best experience.

> *My conclusions:*

And if you've had prior work experience in high school or college, let's add that here:

	Job 1: _____	Job 2: _____	Job 3: _____
What I liked about the job			

	Job 1: _____	Job 2: _____	Job 3: _____
What I didn't like about the job			
What I liked about co-workers and the company			
What I didn't like about co-workers and the company			
What I liked about the culture			

Congratulations! That was a lot of work. What you know now are the ways in which you work best and the environments in which you're most productive. You now have basic guidelines for the kinds of companies you want to pursue.

Based on this information alone, you are *almost* ready to explore internship opportunities through your network and/or school's Career Services Department. But before you get out there, Chapter 2 talks about what is important to employers and how your likes, dislikes, working style, and experience fit into different work environments.

Down and Dirty Recap

- Think of preparing to apply for an internship position as an informed experiment for figuring out what you like to do and how you want to work.
- The "whole you" is what matters to employers. How you spend free time is just as important as how you spend academic time in determining when you're most productive and happy.
- Understanding what you like and don't like will help you develop the right questions to ask in an interview.

What I Know Now (Notes)

What I Need to Do Next (Notes)

CHAPTER 2

What Employers Want

All right, enough about *you*—for the moment. It's time to talk about *them*—your potential employer—and what they want from you as an intern.

What You'll Get From This Chapter

- ✓ We'll figure out the qualities in you that employers value most.
- ✓ We'll add the stories and experiences that speak to your most valuable capabilities. You have them, I promise!
- ✓ We'll get you comfortable with how to talk about your weaker areas and your plan for improvement.

Your stories, experiences, and improvement plans will become another piece of your personal business narrative.

The Big Six

If there is a single word that embodies what employers are looking for in an intern, it's *potential*. Employers look for interns and employees who are curious and willing to grow in these six areas:

1. Teach-ability
2. Adaptability
3. Collaboration
4. Problem solving
5. Humility
6. Leadership

If an employer sees your potential in these areas, you're on your way to an internship.

Since middle school, whether you've known it or not, teachers, professors, and parents have been helping you build these six "21st-century skills." Let's see how you think you stack up.

A Self-Assessment

Your self-assessment against each of the Big Six characteristics becomes the *foundation for conversations with your network of contacts and throughout the interview process.*

Speaking honestly with your potential employer about the skills you bring, where you want to grow, and how you could work with other interns and staff will guide you toward a good "fit."

No one is a rock star in all six areas, and no one knows everything! We all bring different talents to a working environment. So don't be afraid to admit that you are not perfect. Believe it or not, employers *love* to hear your ideas for how you can improve your skills. *Striving to improve is not a sign of weakness*, but an unapologetic demonstration of thoughtful self-awareness. It's also where you can speak to one of the Big Six: *Humility.*

Employers look for people who not only bring skills to a job but also demonstrate the ability and willingness to learn and grow with a company. Interns who quickly learn a company's preferred ways of communicating with staff, clients, and vendors become better integrated into the corporate culture, last longer, and are more successful. This is another one of the Big Six: *Teach-ability.*

Your Strengths and Weaknesses

It's easy and fun to talk about your strengths. Writing them down is an essential first step toward helping your network of friends, family, and teachers work effectively on your behalf. Down the road, this work is guaranteed to make your conversations with potential employers more productive. The same applies to your weaknesses. But in addition to simply writing your weaknesses down, you're also going to develop a plan to address them. By doing so, you're checking two additional areas important to employers: *Critical thinking* and *Communication skills.*

It's *honesty* time!

Here's how to begin your self-assessment:

- Carefully consider your definition of each Big Six characteristic.
- Use the questions under each characteristic as guidelines, but don't be limited by them.
- Use personal examples from your life.
- Although "No experience" answers go in the "Weakness" columns, your ideas for getting more experience in these areas *will be the starting point for embracing improvement and growth.*
- Keep your answers bullet-point brief. *These become foundation statements for your resume and talking points in networking meetings and interviews.*

If you get stuck on a particular subject or topic, ask a teacher, advisor, or someone else who knows you or has worked with you, for perspective and input. Tell that person that you are doing this work *in advance of looking for the best possible internship.* That person will be impressed and will want to help. Later, you can ask that person and others to serve as personal references.

Now it's time to hold a mirror up and have a look at yourself.

My Big Six Assessment

1. TEACH-ABILITY

Learning new techniques and adapting them to the issues presented.
Prompts:
✓ How quickly do I adapt to change?
✓ How do I respond to positive and negative feedback?
 ◦ From peers?
 ◦ From people with authority, such as professors and coaches?
✓ My other ideas: _____

My example of Teach-ability:

My assessment:

2. ADAPTABILITY

The ability to adjust to changing environments, peers, and challenges.

Prompts:

✓ Am I resilient?

✓ How do I react to new challenges?

  ○ Do I welcome them?

  ○ How do I handle the stress?

✓ How do I react to multiple assignments with tough deadlines?

✓ My other ideas: _____

My example of Adaptability:

My assessment:

3. COLLABORATION

The ability to work as part of a team.

Prompts:

✓ Am I more comfortable as a leader or a follower?

✓ How do I feel when I get negative feedback?

  ○ Do I get angry or feel frustrated, disappointed, or confused?

✓ Am I a note-taker or a verbal leader?

✓ My follow-through habits are _____

✓ What is my optimal team environment—small team (fewer than five members), large team (more than five members)?

✓ Would I rather be the most experienced person on a team or the junior member?

✓ My other ideas: _____

My example of Collaboration:

My assessment:

---

4. PROBLEM SOLVING

The mindset to move toward success.

Prompts:

✓ When faced with a *new* challenge, how do I react?

○ Jump in, or stand back and analyze?

✓ Do I offer solutions, even to people who have more authority?

✓ Do I offer to help, even if it is outside my core expertise?

✓ Do I tend to quickly collaborate to solve a problem or try to improve upon a group's initial path toward solutions?

✓ My other ideas: _____

My example of Problem solving:

My assessment:

5. HUMILITY

The ability to be modest and let your actions speak for you.

Prompts:

✓ Am I willing to hear differing points of view?

✓ Do I step back from my idea if someone else has a better point?

✓ How do I react when a solution doesn't include my ideas?

✓ Do I prefer to share credit or "own" a solution?

✓ My other ideas: _____

My example of Humility:

My assessment:

6. LEADERSHIP

The ability to see a big picture and provide direction or guidance.

Prompts:

✓ Do I include others in a problem-solving process?

✓ Do I tend to attack an issue and solve it on my own or seek help and prefer to collaborate?

✓ Do other people look to me for direction?

✓ When things go wrong in group work, what's my first reaction?

  ○ Do it over myself?

  ○ Blame others and walk away?

  ○ Analyze how things went off the rails?

  ○ Figure out who is responsible and ask that they collaborate on a solution?

✓ Do I enjoy working under pressure imposed on me by others?

✓ My other ideas: _____

What All This Says About Me

Good work! You're done! But before you move on, ask yourself, "Was I really honest with myself?" Here's a test: Did you assess yourself as "strong" in every category? If so, then go back and look again at the list. There must be *at least one* area in which you can improve. Find it, or them.

If you feel good about your assessment, you're ready to divide up your strengths and weaknesses.

For your *strongest qualities*, add a real-life story or example. Writing it down here makes it easier to remember and use when you're networking or in an interview.

My three strongest qualities are

1. _____
   Example/story:_____
   _____
   _____

2. _____
   Example/story:_____
   _____
   _____

3. _____
   Example/story:_____
   _____
   _____

How Your Strengths Fit Into Your Personal Business Narrative

Now, look back on what you've just written. You may have worked in a store, become an Eagle Scout, or played on a sports team. What do these examples and stories say about you as a person?

If you've worked in a store, then you have firsthand stories about dealing with customers. This experience could demonstrate your Adaptability, Communication skills, and Humility. If you were an Eagle Scout, your projects can probably demonstrate Leadership, Problem solving, Critical thinking, and Communication. For those on a sports team, tell stories that show Teach-ability, Adaptability, Leadership, and Humility.

Right here is where you start *connecting your experience to what matters to business.* Your stories add memorable details about you and demonstrate potential in the six areas employers value most. They go far to answer *why* a company should hire you to be an intern.

No one overtly says, "I am a humble or teachable person." Your stories prove those qualities. But stories only help you if they are well told. So, practice your stories. Your dog, your parents, your younger brother, or in front of a mirror are all good audiences. It doesn't matter much. Just get comfortable with how your stories fit within your personal narrative. Your ability to talk about and sell your strengths is what will set you apart from other candidates. Your stories are what will be remembered by interviewers.

And now, let's work on the areas to improve.

My three qualities I can improve:

1. _____

2. _____

3. _____

Creating Action Plans for Improvement

Thank you for being honest and listing your weakest areas. Now that you know what they are, let's work on plans to improve. Remember, when the question of your weaknesses comes up during your interview process, *and it will*, it's a prime opportunity to demonstrate at least three of the Big Six qualities the interviewer will be listening for: Humility, Communication, and Teach-ability.

First, prioritize the areas that need the most work. Then, think about what *you can do now* to *begin* improving.

Use the timeline chart given later to establish small, *realistic* goals and deadlines. Making a timeline with small improvement goals creates your accountability to yourself. If you know you're not great with deadlines, tell a friend or advisor about your plan, and ask that person to help you stay on track. There is no need to go it alone! Having other people help you meet your deadlines is quite motivating.

If you get stuck figuring out the activities in the "What Can I Read, Learn, or Do to Improve" section, speak up! Ask for help from a mentor, an advisor, or an insightful friend. Again, there's no need to go it alone and stress out. Keep your plan simple! The more complex your plan, the less likely you will be to work on your weaknesses. After all, the most important part of any improvement is getting started.

My Improvement Plan

Areas I Want to Improve (Weakest to Strongest)	What I Can Read, Learn, or Do to Improve	My Timeline: When I Start, and What Comes First

During an interview, it's good to be able to talk about a plan. But it's much better to have already started working on it. You won't just come across as smart—you'll be seen as humble, proactive, and genuine. Most importantly, you'll be remembered.

Using what you've done in this chapter, when you find yourself in an interview or a networking conversation, you'll be able to focus on *exactly* what's most important for companies. When you are direct about your strengths, you prove *why* you are a good candidate. When you are direct about your weaknesses, you demonstrate maturity. If you show that you have thought through both, you open the door to other questions about the internship program; its projects, roles, and responsibilities; and anything else you would like to know about the company—all valuable information that you could not have found on your own. *For the interviewer, these "next-level" conversations move a person from being just another candidate to being a serious candidate.*

You are off to a great start!

Down and Dirty Recap

Having worked through Chapters 1 and 2, here's what you know about yourself and potential employers:

- What you like to do
- What you don't like to do
- How you work best
- What employers' value
- Your strengths and stories that support your strengths
- Skills that need improvement
- Game plan for improvement
- How all this fits into your personal business narrative

Putting to work what you now know about yourself will help you stand out, be remembered, and rise above the crowd. Your strengths and weaknesses are what make you human and interesting. Don't be afraid to talk about them. For employers, having this insight helps them define *why* they should, or shouldn't, hire you; and *how* you'll contribute.

A company's goal is to hire a balanced, productive team of diverse and complementary skills. Positioning yourself to "fit in, stand out, *and* be teachable" improves your chances of becoming a valuable team member.

What I Know Now (Notes)

What I Need to Do Next (Notes)

CHAPTER 3

Got a Goal?

What You'll Get From This Chapter

The next section is about your goal for an internship. You should have a goal and be able to talk about it with energy, optimism, and clarity. We'll get to all of that as we:

- ✓ Figure out your personal internship goal.
- ✓ Create a preliminary game plan for achieving your goal.
- ✓ Write awesome goal-related questions for your networking conversations and interviews.

Having a clear, well-articulated internship goal has many benefits. A goal does the following:

- Keeps you focused throughout the search process
- Gives the people in your network direction to help you in your search
- Shows employers that you're motivated and thinking about your future
- Becomes an important topic in an interview
- Once hired, serves as a subject for conversations with your supervisor about your responsibilities
- Once hired, serves as a starting point for conversations with your supervisor if your internship ends up not being what you had expected

Declaring a Goal

Let's start by thinking of your goal as a guideline, something for focusing your thinking around what you want to learn or experience during your internship.

Keep it simple. The more complicated the goal, the harder it is to achieve. Plan on having *one very clear goal* for your internship. You'll be learning new things every day, so one goal is enough. If you have too many goals, you'll run the risk of missing the best part of your internship: building new relationships and having fun.

My Goal

Before you can create a goal, you will need some "wants." Below, fill in as many blanks as apply. These will help you organize your thoughts around what you want to achieve and lead you to create a goal that works for you.

Goal Statement Mad Libs

- I want to work in a [size] organization in the _____ business.
- I want to use these parts of my academic major: _____.
- I want to learn how to _____.
- I want to get better at _____.
- I want to meet _____.
- I want to use my _____ skills.

Now, look at everything you wrote down. What's most important? That is your goal for your internship.

Write down your goal. Because when you write it down, it becomes real!

My goal is to complete my internship having accomplished

_____

_____

_____

First Steps Toward Achieving Your Goal

Congratulations! You have a goal!

Now let's figure out what you need to do to get an internship and start achieving your goal. It starts with a Three-Step Game Plan to make your goal statement part of every networking conversation and interview.

Three-Step Game Plan

1. **Make a list of your trusted advisors.**
   These can be coaches, teachers, or adult friends. Once you have the list, prioritize it from the most- to the least-trusted and the most- to the least-connected. You'll want to ask for their opinion of your goal and if they think it's realistic.

2. **Create a timeline for speaking with your advisors.**
   - ✓ It may take time to set up these conversations, so be patient. Plan on putting out lots of requests at the same time.
   - ✓ Consider the first few meetings as practice sessions. It's why you want to begin with your most trusted advisors.
   - ✓ We'll talk about resumes in the next chapter, but make sure you account for the time you will need to produce or update your resume or other supporting materials (e.g., creative portfolio, LinkedIn profile, up-to-date grades).

     If your advisor can meet and your resume isn't ready, have the meeting anyway and explain that your resume is what you'll be working on next. Your advisor may even offer to help!

3. **Practice your goal statement**—*out loud to an audience*! You want to be comfortable and confident when talking about your goal. Pets, stuffed animals, siblings, and parents all are good choices here.

Within each of the three steps, practice is the most important. You'll want to talk about your goal within a natural flow of a conversation. The only way to do that is to practice it out loud and get comfortable saying the words. If you don't practice in advance, there's a good chance, when you do talk about your goal, that it will sound clunky, a little weird, and definitely too scripted. Here are some examples of how to insert a goal into a networking conversation or interview:

- "My goal is to apply in the real world what I am learning in my [insert specific topics/competencies here] major."
- "My internship goal is to learn as much as I can about how a company builds its customer relationships."
- "I would like to find an internship where I have the chance to practice public speaking."

Goal-Related Questions

Once you are comfortable talking about your goal, you'll want to be ready with follow-up questions for both your network and your interviews. Your thoughtful questions will position you to your network and interviewers as a serious candidate. And the answers you get will go far in determining if that place is a place where you want to intern.

Follow-up questions to the "public speaking" goal (from earlier) might sound like the following:

- Where might there be opportunities for public speaking?
- Is there an intern project that requires a presentation at the end?
- Who is the audience for that presentation?
- If there isn't a project that involves a formal presentation, are there other opportunities to practice this skill?
- Do you have any public speaking advice?

Your specific goal will determine the questions you'll ask. But *always, always, always ask for people's opinion and advice!* People love to talk about themselves and asking for advice gives them a chance to tell you what they know. After all, your network and your interviewer have more business and company experience than you do. You can learn a lot from asking them, "What do you think?"

Here is a simple way to organize your thoughts and develop your questions so that every conversation becomes a productive conversation.

My goal is

_____

_____

To achieve my goal, I would like to do the following things during an internship:

1. _____
2. _____
3. _____

These are questions I want to ask my network or interviewer to better understand if I can achieve my goal during the internship:

1. _____
2. _____
3. _____

You should expect follow-up questions. You want more questions.

More Questions = More Opportunities to Leave a Great Impression

The most basic question you can expect is "Beyond your goal, what else do you want to get out of an internship?" But what you're really being asked, what the interviewer really wants to know, is how your goal connects with company needs! And as much as you'd like to say "Get paid, and put a great line on my resume," you can't. Even though it may be true, it tells the interviewer nothing about you or what you'll bring to the company.

Your best answer is a combination of two great words: What you can contribute and what you'd like to learn. You can do the following:

1. Answer with a story that describes a learning moment and how you've applied that learning—but make it short and be _very_ clear!
2. Answer with a description of the strengths and skills you bring to their business challenges and what you want out of the experience.

Other follow-up questions you can expect include these:

- Do you think you can accomplish your goal in 6 to 10 weeks?
- What are you doing in advance to prepare?
- If you don't get in here or we can't help you achieve your goal, what is your "plan B?"

We'll go over all of these, and many more, in Chapter 6 on interviewing.

Now you have a goal, a game plan, and follow-up questions. We'll end the chapter with a real-life story about how having a goal worked for one intern.

This Really Happened

Alyssa was a college junior faced with choosing between two internships in her chosen field of political science. The first was with a big, well-known public relations firm specializing in political campaigns. Alyssa would be working with a large team on a campaign and responsible for coordinating schedules and press appearances.

The second was working for a first-time, unknown candidate on her campaign for Congress. Alyssa would be doing "anything and everything" from scheduling press interviews to coordinating speaking engagements, meeting with supporters, and ordering lunches. In both cases, her days would be long and intense.

Alyssa's parents liked the name recognition and network opportunities of the big PR firm. Alyssa agreed but was intrigued by the "anything and everything" of working for an unknown.

What Would You Do? Why? How Would You Decide?

This is Alyssa's decision.

In conversations with her advisors, she said, "My internship goal is to see political science in practice, not just as academic theory. I have two great but very different opportunities. I could use your help deciding which to choose." She developed a list of pros and cons and asked follow-up questions of each employer. Ultimately, she chose the candidate position because it came closest to her goal of learning about politics at a grassroots level.

What makes this an important story is how Alyssa explained her decision to the big PR firm. After turning down the big firm, she wanted to be sure that they thought well enough about her to agree to "stay in touch."

No one likes being rejected, especially a company that is offering an internship position; so Alyssa practiced what she knew would be a difficult conversation. She made sure that the big PR firm understood her goal and the rationale behind her decision to intern for the candidate. The big firm agreed to stay in touch. And during her senior year, Alyssa and the big firm discussed a full-time, entry-level position.

Decision Making Made Easier

Once you begin researching companies, you'll find many opportunities worthy of exploration. Keep track of everything you learn, in writing, especially the following information:

1. Your network's advice about the opportunity
2. Your list of pros and cons about the company
3. Key takeaways from each interview and conversation
4. How each opportunity connects with your goal

Finding the right internship can take a while and may involve a lot of details. Having notes about what happened in the moment can help you later.

Down and Dirty Recap

- A goal gives you direction and purpose.
- A goal helps the people in your network focus their connections on your behalf.
- A goal helps guide your interview questions.

The two primary concerns of any company are (1) hiring the right people and (2) being productive and profitable. Having a goal and connecting it with their business allow interviewers and employers to "see" where you will fit in as an intern.

What I Know Now (Notes)

What I Need to Do Next (Notes)

CHAPTER 4

The Three Versions of You

Now that you understand more about why internships are important and how to set goals for your experience, it's time to begin the search process. Finding the right internship is a combination of researching companies, networking, and interviewing. In Chapter 2, you completed self-assessments for determining what kinds of organizations to research. That's a great start. Now it's time to do a deeper dive, prepare to get in front of people, and tell your story.

When you are networking and interviewing, there are three versions of you that your network connection or interviewer wants to see:

The Paper You—that's your resume.
The Online You—that's you on LinkedIn and other social media.
The In-Person You—that's you in meetings and interviews.

To tell a compelling and consistent story, all three must connect.

What You'll Get From This Chapter

This chapter is about putting together a paper resume that won't put a reader to sleep and about building an online presence that tells your story. Developing these tools will prepare you for the in-person networking conversations and interviews to come.

Why Resumes and LinkedIn Profiles Are Valuable

For employers, resumes and LinkedIn profiles deliver the following:

- A quick overview of your experience and academics without requiring a phone call or in-person conversation

- A glimpse into your personality, how you organize information, and what's important to you
- A convenient document to review, comment on, and, hopefully, pass along to colleagues
- A tool for comparing candidates
- The basis for preparing interview questions

For an intern candidate, a resume is where you can:

- Organize your experience.
- Focus your thinking on *who* you are, *what* you've done, and *how* you work.
- Identify themes in your experience and organize stories to share with your network and relate in an interview.
- Use numbers to explain the depth of your experience and why it matters.
- Add personal details that create connections with your reader.
- Connect *your* experience with a *business's* needs and goals.

The bottom line is that a great resume and online profile describe a person anyone would want to meet. Think of the exercises as creating a profile that leads to a fun first date.

If you think about a first date, it's all about making a positive first impression and telling stories people remember. This is also what a great resume or online profile delivers. It tells the reader just enough but, like a great first date, leaves the reader wanting to know more.

That's when you get a second date—in business, that's an interview. *And if you get the interview, your resume and LinkedIn profile have done their job.*

Let's talk about your paper resume.

The Paper You: Putting Together a Mighty Resume

Your resume has to leave a great first impression. Have you ever heard the expression "Everything communicates"? When it comes to your resume, the job of every word, idea, or phrase is to lead the reader to want to meet you. If your resume is boring, the reader will assume you're boring. No one wants to interview a boring person.

But wait!! Employers hire people, not paper.

That's true. *But they see the paper first* and, as unfair as it may seem, they *will* eliminate you if they don't like your paper!

By the end of this section, you'll have a paper resume that:

- Makes a great first impression
- Let's your personality shine through
- Connects your experience with what business cares about
- Gets you an interview

When you're putting together any resume, here are three big-picture guidelines to keep in mind. They involve three qualities: knowledge, personality, and "fit":

1. *Knowledge*: "What do I want my reader to know about me?" If you communicate three unique or memorable facts, the resume has done its job.
2. *Personality*: "Which parts of my personality do I want to highlight?" An intern program at a sports team will look for different personality traits than an analytics-heavy program.
3. *Fit*: "How do I match up with the job description?" Your resume should speak directly to *both* what the company is looking for *and* what you want for yourself. If you are excited by the work, make sure that your resume highlights things you have done or skills you've used that speak directly to what the employer wants.

If you already have a resume, see how it stacks up against the following criteria. Does your resume:

- Explain what drives *you*?
- Create a theme that connects your academics, summer jobs, hobbies, and experiences?

- Articulate your goals, aspirations, and dreams?
- Talk about the skills you offer and what you want to learn?
- Communicate that you have a personality and are human?

If your current resume is lacking, let's fix it or build a new one that gets you an interview. What you'll end up with is a resume that you can customize based on specific opportunities and intern program descriptions. Be patient. It takes a while to get this right, but it will be worth the time.

A Mighty Resume in Three Easy Steps

1. *Outline*: Start by writing down *everything you've done* that might be important. This will be put into categories a little later in the chapter.
2. *Enhance with metrics and themes*: Connect what you have done, where you have worked, and what you have studied with metrics, your passions, and interests. These larger themes give your reader insight into your personality.
3. *Test*: Ask your advisors to review your resume to make sure that what you're saying tells the best story of you.

Step 1: Outline

Writing an outline focuses your thinking and makes it easier to create connections with the reader. The outline is made up of a header, a summary, and your experience.

What to Include in Your Resume Outline

✓ Header—Name, phone number, e-mail address, LinkedIn profile
   Add a photo (optional): People connect with faces they see. (No supercasual photos, please!)

For creative position resumes: Link to your videos, work samples, and personal website.

Note: There is a section at the end of this chapter on video resumes, but this basic outline remains the same.

✓ Summary—A few sentences that tie together your experience, passion, and goals. This will be supported further in the "Experience" section of your outline.

What to Include in a Memorable Summary

You already have all the elements you need to write a summary. Use what you learned in Chapters 1 through 3 to answer these prompts. Each prompt will become a summary sentence.

Who you are: Identify the larger theme of what you like to do, for example, building things, exploring, and solving problems.

What you do: Your interests and passions and how these are supported by your academics and other experience.

Why this benefits your employer: Connect your goals and skills with why you believe you would be valuable as an intern.

If this sounds confusing, here is an example:

I love playing guitar and relate to music's structure and freedom to experiment. Academically, computer science and environmental science are my focus. My goal is to work with people using technology creatively to address our environmental challenges.

If you are having trouble including your goal in your summary, this Mad Lib will help:

My goal is to [choose a verb, e.g., "help," "support," or "assist"] *to* [insert the benefit for the company] *and* [choose a verb, e.g., "improve," "learn," "do"] *to* [insert the benefit for yourself].

Keep your sentences short and clear. *Every word should have a purpose* and support your theme. Avoid a laundry list of activities separated by commas.

✓ Your Experience—The categories given here will help organize your thoughts. Add relevant information to each bulleted item. Write down anything that comes to mind. You can shorten the list later:
  • Academic areas of study
  • Prior internships (include dates of internship)
  • Prior jobs (include dates of employment)
  • Extended travel with service programs or work/study programs (include dates)
  • Volunteer work (include dates)
  • Education (include dates and intended graduation date)
  • Extracurricular club activities (include dates of participation)
  • Proficiencies and certifications (include dates of certification)
  • Personal passions and interests

Use what's in your "Experience" section to test your summary. Your "Experience" section should support what you wrote. If your "Experience" section doesn't support your summary, then revise your summary to reflect your experience.

Step 2: Enhance With Metrics and Themes

Now that you have a summary and have listed all your experience and passions to date, it's time to boost these two sections with metrics and themes that will let your winning personality shine through.

Enhance Your Resume With Metrics—Because Numbers
Don't Lie

Employers love metrics, whole numbers and percentages. Metrics add depth and credibility to your experience. Prior internships, prior jobs, volunteer work, extracurricular activities, clubs, passions, and interests are all areas that lend themselves well to adding metrics. Use numbers to clarify both the scope and the results of what you've done. Use as many metrics as you can.

Example of How to Use Metrics

If you worked in a retail store, connect and quantify your sales experience with what you learned about customer service. Where you can, connect with a Big Six trait.

Note: Don't include the Big Six trait by name when you are writing your resume. The traits are shown here just to illustrate wording that supports a Big Six quality.

For retail experience, metrics may sound like the following:

Served an average of 150 customers a day, treating all courteously and efficiently [Humility]

Formed strong relationships with three-person management team, from my supervisor to the department's senior vice president [Collaboration]

Developed a customer's return rate of 70 percent [Problem solving]

Are your metrics "meh" or "mighty"? Consider the examples given next to assess the strength of the metrics in your resume.

Meh Metric. Summer 2016: Joe's Ice Cream, Anytown, USA, for six weeks. Server and cleanup crew. [14 words]

This example reports only the facts and offers a weak metric (six weeks). It offers no insight into what you learned from the experience.

Mighty Metric. Summer 2016: Joe's Ice Cream, Anytown, USA. Counter server; maintained highest cleanliness standard. Hundreds of happy, returning customers. (18 words)

This is a mighty example because it communicates, in fewer words:

✓ A *stronger* metric—*hundreds*
✓ Your *positive* attitude

✓ The *pride* you took in your work
✓ An understanding of *customer loyalty*

These are all valuable qualities that employers look for in interns. And you have communicated four important aspects of yourself in only 18 words!

Enhance Your Resume by Creating Themes

Look at what you included in your experience lists. This is where you can create themes that tell an employer more about you and your personality. Don't downplay any past experience. Babysitting, lifeguarding, and working in a shop all show direct work experience and the ability to communicate, adapt, learn, and act responsibly and in a trustworthy manner.

Even if you haven't held a job before, chances are you are involved with a club, play a sport, belong to a fraternity or sorority, or participate in any number of other campus-related activities. Your activities set you apart and are an important addition to your resume. The first step is to look at the list of your activities. The second step is to figure out the defining theme that pulls your activities together. The activities support the theme, and the theme is what is most important to communicate. Creating themes says a lot about you and your personality.

Example of How to Develop a Theme

If you are a member of the women's rugby team, sing backup in a band, and tutor local girls in math, you can tie all those elements together under a central theme in your resume's "Personal Passions and Interests" section. This is an example of how to unify all your activities:

On the field, the stage, and classroom, I strive to make women and girls more confident and competitive.
   Member, Women's Rugby team
   Member, Math Girls Club
   One of three female backup singers—R&B band

By explaining your interests within a larger context, you're making a powerful, personal statement that shows self-awareness and larger purpose. Employers appreciate and look for this insight. Developing one or two themes will set you apart from your competition.

Enhance Your Resume With Proficiencies

This is an important section. List any areas in which you consider yourself proficient. When writing this section, consider which skills your potential employer will value, and order your proficiencies accordingly.

Note: Certification in Excel or Adobe Photoshop is a proficiency. Unless you are an acknowledged social media influencer and getting an internship that leverages your influence, your personal Facebook, Instagram, or Twitter usage is not considered a proficiency.

If you think you are coming up short on this list, consider getting certified in Excel or some other widely valued program. These certification programs are inexpensive, and many are available online.

If you've signed up for or are currently pursuing a certification, list it here. It signals to employers that you're proactively building your skills. For example:

Excel Certification—in progress. Estimated completion: [date]

Make Every Word Count

One page is not a lot of space to tell your whole story. That means you'll need to avoid cluttering your resume with unnecessary words. Be sure to do the following:

- Delete pronouns—"you," "me," "her," "he," and so on.
- Delete filler words—"and," "then," "as," and "resulting in."
- Use verbs and action words—"addressed," "balanced," "developed," "marketed," "estimated," "planned," and "prepared" to accurately describe your contribution.

It can be a challenge to be clear and get your personality across in a few words, but it's what your employer expects. Being clear now will also help when you get to the interview. Think of it as getting ready for that second date. It takes time in the beginning, but the result is often worth the effort.

Customizing a General Resume

Now that you have a solid general resume—a header, summary, and "Experience" and "Proficiencies" sections, all enhanced with metrics, themes, and stories—let's customize your resume to specific internship opportunities.

The most important guideline to remember is to always write with your reader in mind. Look for places where you can connect your experiences to the skills that employers value. Order your experience to align with what's most important in the job description.

If a job description uses phrases like "self-starter," "good communicator," or "team player," your resume must include examples that demonstrate you possess these characteristics.

If you are a marketing major with a math minor and applying to a data-centric internship, lead with your math and technical skills and include examples of how you have used these skills in a marketing exercise.

If you are applying to a marketing internship, emphasize your marketing classes and connect your relationship-building activities with clubs, events, and prior work experience.

Industry-focused resumes with examples of your experience and classwork demonstrate genuine interest and will help your reader see how you fit in as an intern. It's a little more work to customize your resumes, but it is worth it in the end.

Your Resume Format

Now you are ready to make your resume pretty and test it with your advisors. Please don't overcomplicate or get hung up on the format. A resume's job is to communicate information and get you the interview, not to wow your reader with your ability to format text.

There are many resume formats available online. A simple Google search will yield a long list. Find a format that best reflects your personality and showcases your experience and accomplishments. But make sure the format you choose allows you to put all the most important information on one page—while using an 11- or 12-point font. Don't make your reader struggle with small print. If it's hard to read, it will end up in the discard pile.

As an aside, I know that distilling your many different experiences, hobbies, and goals down to one page can feel demeaning. Many people think "There's just no way I can communicate everything about myself in just one page. There's so much more to who I am."

Bad news—tough. A resume is the most basic tool of interviewing, and everyone eventually has to write one.

Good news—although it may feel like it, you're not reducing everything about who you are to just one page. Think of your resume as a springboard to help you and your interviewer have an informed conversation about each other. Crafting a narrative that's clear, concise, and consistent in direction helps you guide the conversation where you want it to go. Plus, everyone must write a resume at some point—people get it. We will talk about how to make that connection between the paper and in-person you in the next chapter.

Step 3: Test

Three Tests: How I Know My Resume Will Stand Out

Once your resume is written, it's time to take it on the road and test it out.

Test #1: "Did I Include the Best Information?"

For this test, you'll want to have someone who knows you well, a family member or adult friend, read and critique your resume. Have that person use the prompts given next as a guide to tell you if you left anything out:

- "Was my resume easy to read and follow?"
- "Did the resume 'sound like me'?"

- "Did my experience support my summary statement?"
- "Have I clearly said what I've studied and done, and communicate what I want to do next?"
- "Did I include my goal?"
- "Did the 'Personal Passions and Interests' section add insight into how I might be valuable as an intern?"
- "Is there anything about the resume that doesn't make sense?"
- "Did I leave anything out?"
- "After reading my resume, what would you repeat about me?"

If you don't like the feedback you get, revise what wasn't well received. If a reader who already knows you is confused, you can assume the resume reviewer will also be confused.

Test #2: The "Five What's" Test

This test is for one of your trusted advisors, someone outside of your immediate family and circle of friends. Answers to the following five questions will tell you if your personality has come through and if you've connected what you've done to what's important for business:

1. "What do I now know about this person?"
2. "What is one memorable part of the resume?"
3. "What skills support the person's experience?"
4. "What do I want to know more about?"
5. "What is not clear?"

Test #3: "Is My Resume Meh or Mighty?"

This is a test for you to determine if you've done all you can to make your resume memorable. Answer these four questions:

1. **"Is my resume a list or a story?"**
   A. A *meh* resume *lists* your experience and academic achievements. Nice, but kind of dull.
   B. A **mighty** resume *tells the story* of your experiences and *conveys confidence and optimism.* Interesting, and more memorable!

2. **"Is my resume a chronology or a theme?"**

    A. A *meh* resume *gives a* chronology of information. Technically accurate, but hardly unusual.

    B. A **mighty** resume *unifies* your experience around a central theme and presents you as a person with passion and focus.

3. **"Is my resume a proficiency list, or does it describe the value of my proficiencies?"**

    A. A *meh* resume *ticks off* proficiencies that an employer may find useful but fails to make a strategic connection to a company's goals.

    B. A **mighty** resume *connects* your skills and interests to an employer's needs. If your assertion of what the employer needs is off base, you'll still get credit for trying.

4. **"Is my resume a list of facts, or does it have personality?"**

    A. A *meh* resume communicates a checklist of facts.

    B. A **mighty** resume has *personality.* It allows the reader to "see" your personality and how you will contribute to the organization.

And finally, after all the writing, editing, reviewing, repaginating, and proofreading, and *BEFORE* SENDING IT OUT, SAVE IT AS A PDF!

    A PDF is the *only* version you will *ever send out.*

You don't want this to happen to you.

This Really Happened

Sebastian was a business major looking for an internship in finance. He put together a new resume and was excited to get feedback from his friends, family, and school advisors. With confidence, he sent his resume to everyone he trusted. And using "Track Changes," everyone in his network came through with great suggestions, edits, questions, and personal comments.

Sebastian made some tweaks and saved the "final" document. Then, with hope and optimism, he confidently sent his resume to a long list of his top prospective employers.

Nothing happened. He didn't get a single response. Not one.

About three weeks later, a sympathetic HR manager called Sebastian. She explained that she had received his resume but could not seriously consider him as a candidate.

Unknowingly, the "final" document Sebastian had sent out to his top prospects included every "Track Change" edit that he and his network had made to his resume.

Sebastian was mortified. Now, his top 10 firms wouldn't consider him for an internship. He called all the firms to explain, but in a competitive internship environment, the firms had already moved on to other candidates. Sebastian was left with only a few options at far less prestigious companies.

Sebastian's Mistake Is Avoidable—Here's What to Do

1. Accept (or reject) "Track Changes" and save the document with a unique name and date. Mark your resume FINAL.
2. Print out your resume and review it for content, tracking, pagination, sentence alignment, and typos.
3. Test the pagination: Send as a PDF and a Word document to other devices to see how it formats, both electronically and when printed. Include a PC, Mac, iPad, and at least one phone in your test.

And always save your resume two ways:

1. Save it as a Word document for you to edit and customize for different opportunities.
2. Save it as a PDF to send to employers.

If You Are Putting Together a Video Resume

The type of internship you are looking for will determine if a video resume or a paper resume is most appropriate. For example, if you are applying to a film editing company, tech company, video company, mobile-based business, or creative division of an advertising agency, a video resume may be more appropriate. A video resume allows employers to see you and appreciate your personality, while you get to talk about your goals and show work samples.

If you decide to produce a video, include within your video resume what would normally be contained within your cover letter. Write out a script and practice. Follow the outline we talked about earlier in the chapter. The flow of information should be the same as with a paper resume with one exception. At the end of your short video, you can ask for an interview!

The Online You: LinkedIn—A Must Do, and Other Social Media

Everything you've done for your paper resume and narrative can be used to build or improve your LinkedIn profile. If you're not on LinkedIn already, you will need to build a profile. It's a must.

Getting Noticed on LinkedIn

Because you're probably on Facebook, you may have decided to look for an internship through your Facebook network. That's not a bad idea, but don't limit yourself to just Facebook. Facebook has been working hard to compete with LinkedIn as an employment site. And Facebook is getting better all the time. But for the business sector, LinkedIn is where business gets done.

Use LinkedIn to build your network for your internship so you'll have a presence when you start your full-time job search. Here are three pointers for using LinkedIn:

1. *Use LinkedIn to build your professional network.* This platform will allow you to connect with people at your target companies, introduce yourself, and start a conversation. It's a valuable tool for both Automatics and Nonautomatics.
2. *Learn the functionality of LinkedIn.* It's constantly improving, and the tutorials are easy to use. Check them out.
3. *Sign up for internship and job alerts through the Student Jobs Portal and from company websites.* The search engine optimization function of LinkedIn pushes postings that match your profile.

How to Use LinkedIn to Start Conversations

First, build a LinkedIn profile and include a photo, and follow these six guidelines:

1. *Write a clear profile descriptor.* Your LinkedIn descriptor (right under your name and photo) tells others who you are, what you have done, and, most importantly, your employment goals. Putting this information in the descriptor helps the LinkedIn search engines push relevant connections and opportunities to your profile. Example of a LinkedIn descriptor: Student-Athlete/Finance Major Seeking Internship in Sports Management.

2. *Use the "Summary" space wisely.* Expand on your three-sentence resume summary. Add more details and stories to make it more interesting. All the same strategies you've been following in the preceding chapters apply here. Connect with the Big Six and let your personality shine through. One paragraph, consisting of six to eight sentences, is long enough.

3. *Build your connections.* Connect with as many people as possible in your areas of interest. As a guide, a "500+ Connections" profile has more credibility than a "47 Connections" profile, so get out there and make requests! Connections are another path for the search engines to push employment opportunities to your profile. Prospective connections will often look at your profile to see whom they already know before connecting with you. When you have more connections, it's easier to add connections. Start today.

When you make a request to connect, add a custom note introducing yourself, telling the connection you are interested in pursuing internship opportunities, and would like to connect so you can learn more about their experience and the company. A custom note gets better results than a request made with no context. Most businesspeople are interested in helping those new to the field. Your request gives them that opportunity.

4. *Ask for recommendations.* Potential employers read recommendations! Request recommendations from teachers, coaches, and past employers—anyone professional you know who is also on LinkedIn.

Recommendations are your personal Yelp review and give insight into your work habits and personality. Both are important, because employers hire interns for both skill and fit.

5. *Join industry-specific LinkedIn groups and start conversations with the members.* Create an online presence and a point of view by making informed comments or asking questions on conversations within the group. This will help you get noticed.

   Hint: Don't just "Like" a group conversation. Say something to add to the conversation or ask a question to begin a new conversation.

   You'll also want to stay up to date with industry trends and industry research before your interview. Belonging to industry-specific groups is a great way to learn about what's trending in an industry. The more active you are on LinkedIn, the more recognizable you become to employers when you begin your internship search.

6. *Upload your PDF resume. Do not include any personal information, such as your address or phone number, on the resume you post on LinkedIn or any social media platform including Indeed or Facebook!* Sadly, there are creepy people out there, even on LinkedIn. Just include your e-mail.

A note about your e-mail address: Have an e-mail address that includes your name and sounds professional. For example: johnsmith92@gmail.com, not beerpong92@gmail.com.

Include your name as part of your e-mail address so connections and potential employers can easily associate you with your correspondence. Don't make people work too hard to connect you with your e-mail address.

Final Note: What Your Social Media Says About You

The world is connected. What you may not know is that if you are seriously being considered for a position, employers may scrape the Web to piece together your online picture. This may or may not happen at the internship stage, but it will likely happen when you look for a full-time job, so you might as well start now. Look carefully at all of your social media accounts for any photos or statements you've made that potential employers might find inappropriate. Your goal is to be consistent across your resume, cover letter, and social media platforms. Too many "red cup" photos? Start deleting.

And finally, if there is something on the Web that you are not especially proud of, be prepared to talk about it should it come up in an interview.

The In-Person You: Connecting the Paper You and the Online You With the Actual You

Congratulations! You've distilled your experience down to one page!

Now it's time to think about the stories you'll tell your network and interviewer to support what you've said. Stories are important, because *people may not remember facts, but they* will *remember a story.* Your stories will set you apart.

Make sure that your stories:

- Are as clear and concise as your resume
- Directly support your experience
- Speak to what the employer values and wants

Connect Your Stories to the Big Six

Think about the stories that support the experience, past jobs, activities, and/or proficiencies on your resume. Then, connect those stories with the Big Six or a specific and relevant skill.

Think about your stories in terms of the following five elements:

1. Success
2. Failure
3. Lessons learned
4. Lessons applied (at school, at home, with friends, at another job)
5. How lessons learned connect to the internship you want

Draft an outline of your story. Use bullet points to address some or all of the areas earlier.

Remember that you'll often be telling your story to a professional listener. So, you will need to practice. A lot. Tell your story out loud. How does it sound? If you were a listener, would the story be interesting to you? What is memorable?

Ask adults for feedback and constructive criticism.

Finally, be humble when you tell your stories. No matter how great your success, there's always room to improve.

Great job! That was a lot of work. The next step is to get it out there in the world so you can start evaluating different opportunities. Before you attach your resume to job applications, it's time to meet with your network—your guides for finding your best possible internship.

That's what's next.

Down and Dirty Recap

- Make sure the Paper You, Online You, and In-Person You tell the same story.
- Create a LinkedIn profile.
- Make your resume and LinkedIn profile easy to read for the reviewer.
- Connect what you have already done with what you want to do.
- Add personal details.
- Tie it all together with an awesome summary.
- Connect your experience to what matters to employers.
- Test what you've written.
- Figure out the stories that support your experience.
- Check your social media.

Finally, please don't exaggerate on your resume. Good recruiters and interviewers will see right through it. You'll never know why you didn't get the internship. You just won't get a call back.

What I Know Now (Notes)

What I Need to Do Next (Notes)

CHAPTER 5

Getting Your Network Working for You

What You'll Get From This Chapter

This chapter connects the Paper You with the In-Person You. With your network and in interviews, you'll be prepared to talk about yourself clearly and explain why you'll be a great intern. Here's what we'll cover:

- ✓ Identifying who's in your network and how they can help
- ✓ Requesting help with dignity and confidence
- ✓ Getting your network to say what you want them to say about you
- ✓ Asking the right questions
- ✓ Researching potential internships
- ✓ Having the conversations that lead to action

At some point in your career, you'll likely get a job through your network. Chances are it will be a great job. Here's proof: The 2022 Job Seeker Nation Report found that 70 percent of all job seekers got their "favorite or best job" from connections in their networks. Getting an internship is no different. Why? Because you know and trust the people in your network and they, with the right guidance from you, are willing to help.

The people in your network are interested in your success. Your network will offer valuable insight into why an employer should hire you, work–life balance, and how you will fit in. The people in your network will want to share their advice and guidance and talk about their experiences. Let them.

People in your network can help you by sharing their positive impression of you with their trusted business colleagues. They provide the beyond-the-resume information about your personality, character, and work ethic that employers want to know. Your job is to be smart about how you *engage with your network*.

Here is where you put all of the tools and the narrative you've built in Chapters 1 through 4 to work and give your contacts the information and *guidance they need* to make the *introductions you want*.

When to Start Networking

Internships get snapped up quickly. Begin your internship-planning conversations as early as you can, but certainly no later than September or October for the following summer. If you're applying to an internship in the financial or tech sectors, your planning conversations should begin the prior January. Internships in this area are usually filled by October for a June start.

"What If I Don't Have a Network?"

Unless you have spent the last 18 years in a cave, you do have a network. Everyone has a network. Begin with the people closest to you and build out your list of contacts. As you go through, be open to people's ideas and feedback. If you have a very specific vision and people don't have contacts at your "dream" internship, don't despair—part of the internship process is to develop experience that could be valuable once you land in that dream job (in either a different department or company). Every opportunity can be valuable—if you let it.

"Who Are My Contacts?"

The Low-Hanging Fruit: Friends and Family

This is the easiest place to start. Friends and family want you to succeed. So don't be shy about asking them for help. *This is not a sign of weakness!*

Some of your family and friends may remember you as that "cute little kid." Your job is to bring them up to date about you as an adult. Your conversations must give them the information they need to describe you to *their* colleagues and connections as an emerging professional.

Make a list of where your family and friends work. This will help you see the types of businesses and sectors where your network can offer information and make introductions.

The Next Best Ones: Guidance or Career Services Counselors

The folks in your school's Career Services Department are a great resource. Most have relationships with companies and know about internship opportunities.

They can help direct your search. Most schools have a database of available internships. Start by looking through the database and listing interesting opportunities.

If you don't know where you want to start, share the results of your "How I Work" chart and your internship goal with Career Services. Bring a copy of your general resume and walk your counselor through your experience, skills, and proficiencies. Work with your counselor to find opportunities that would be a good match. Talking to your counselor is also a great place to test out your stories.

Everyone Else: Other People in Your Network

Think about your industry-focused professors, past employers, community business owners, coaches, and other influential adults in your world. Don't be afraid to reach out. They'll be flattered, and meeting with you gives them the opportunity to offer advice. And always, always thank these people for their help, both verbally and with a short, handwritten note. That means you will need to buy yourself a box of inexpensive but attractive stationery.

Work the Internet

Once you have built your LinkedIn profile, start making connections in areas that are interesting and that seem to need the skills you have. Don't be afraid to explore businesses outside your comfort area. For example, if you are a data analytics major, don't only look at "pure-play" analytics firms. Every business runs and makes decisions based on data. Consider industries or organizations that seem interesting and also depend on data. Remember the movie *Moneyball*? The work you did in Chapters 1 and 2 identifying your interests, passions, and skills will help you expand your thinking.

This is a great opportunity to combine and apply your academic and free-time interests and apply them to a business environment. Explore! There are a lot of businesses doing cool work out there.

Help Your Network Help You

The goal of networking is to move you toward the companies that offer a great fit. In your networking meetings, talk about what you developed in Chapters 1 through 4:

- "How I Work" profile of what you like to do and how you work best
- Ideas about the types of companies to explore
- Strongest skills
- Areas to improve
- Your internship goal
- Your resume that connects experience to what employers value
- Your LinkedIn profile and industry-specific connections

You can use the chart given later to organize the information. It will allow you to quickly access the profile you want others to see and hear about. If you are good with graphics, you can also turn this into an infographic to share with your network.

How I Work

How I work best	Ideal sector(s)	Ideal company size	My strongest skills	My areas for improvement	My internship goal

Now, it's time to prepare for a productive networking conversation.

Learn About Your Networking Contact

As you develop your list of target companies, and in advance of your networking conversations, spend time researching the company where your contact works. A 15-minute read of the company's website will give you a sense of the company's culture and the way in which it operates. Here are some things to look for when you are researching a company:

Mission: Be sure to read a company's mission statement and business objectives. Research their involvement in the community to see if what they are doing aligns with what is important to you.

Values: Find the company's "values" statement. Think about it and ask yourself if your values align with the company's. Carefully examine how the company integrated its values into its descriptions of open positions. This will tell you a lot about how the company sees itself, how it wants to be seen, and how it regards its employees. In short, company culture.

Senior staff: Google senior executives. Read their biographies and understand the path they took to get to the company. Look for areas of commonality and write down questions you have about their path and work. That information will come in handy during the interviewing process. Learning about senior management will give you additional insight into the culture of the company and the employee characteristics that the company hires for and values.

General Networking Meeting Guidelines

In meetings, the first question you're likely to hear is "What do you want to do?" It's here that you can direct your network toward an industry or a company. And you'll want to explain why. The profile you just built and your resume will help guide the conversation.

Offer as much input as possible about your skills and goals. This will make your network's task of referring you easier. And the people in your network will appreciate your effort and thought! Even if they can't get you closer to your ideal company, remain open to hearing what they have to say. Your contacts just might have ideas that you haven't considered.

React in a positive way to what you hear. Remember that people may see something in you that you don't see in yourself. Before jumping in to ask for a referral or an introduction, ask for feedback on the information you've given:

- What questions do they have?
- Is there anything they don't understand?

Keep track of your conversations. You are busy doing a lot of things—school, extracurricular activities, and now networking. After a while, it can be hard to remember individual conversations. Use this spreadsheet to keep track of your networking conversations.

My Networking Spreadsheet

Contact Name	
Occupation	
Industry	
First Meeting Date	
Result	
Next Steps Me/Them	
Second Meeting/ Conversation Date	
Next Steps Me/Them	
Comments	

Preparing for Networking Conversations

Because you have limited work experience, your first ask should be for advice.

People love to give advice. Create context by explaining the kind of person and worker you are and how you will be valuable as an intern. This ask will help you explore possibilities together.

Having a successful networking conversation takes preparation. Here's how to have a successful conversation:

- Practice *out loud* how you will *begin* the conversation. ***First impressions matter.*** (See the conversation starters given later.)
- Have stories ready to give depth to your experience.
- Identify four or five questions you would like to ask about internship opportunities, but stay flexible as the conversation evolves.
- Go in with an idea of the help you want, but again, stay flexible. An offer of help may not emerge until you are well into your conversation.
- Prepare specific questions about your contact's company or the industry in which your contact works.

A word about nonverbal skills. During networking conversations, whether in person or online, it's important to show your executive presence—that's your confident, professional persona. Executive presence is made up of good eye contact, clear and concise speaking, and a confident manner. Practicing what you want to say in advance of a meeting helps you hone these skills and prepare to calmly answer questions you may not be expecting.

If you are networking remotely, so tips to remember: leave you camera on; make sure you are in a quiet, well-lit room with a neutral background, sitting at a desk or table. It should not be a public space where people could be coming and going—— no matter how quiet it *usually* is, try not to tempt fate. Dress in a business shirt. Check the volume level in advance and use earbuds or headphones to minimize background noise. One final pro-tip- sign into the call 5 minutes early. It's a small detail that leaves a big positive impression.

Conversation Starters That Always Work

Here are some conversation starters to get your networking off to a great start. Ask your contact:

- "How did you get started in your field?"
- "What was your overall career path?"
- "What was your best or favorite job? Why?"
- "Were there any specific classes you took in school that helped you in your job?"
- "Are there any classes you *wished* you had taken to better prepare you for your role?"
- "Did you ever have an internship? What was your experience?"
- "I am not sure where I would like to work, but I liked what I saw about [XX] [culture, business goals, products, etc.] on [XX] Company's website. Do you know anything about [XX] or any organizations that are similar?"
- "What is your advice for getting started in the [XX] industry?"

These conversation starters will help your contact focus on his or her advice and offer appropriate introductions or referrals. Even if nothing comes from this networking meeting, your preparation work will impress your contact, leave a positive impression, and maybe lead to future conversations about other positions.

Plan on taking a few notes in the meeting. Notes will help you organize your conversations and plan your follow-up questions. Remember, it's a conversation, not a class. Stay fully engaged, visually and verbally.

If your contact has agreed to make an introduction on your behalf, ask your contact what he or she can tell you about that person.

Conversation Dos and Don'ts

People want to help you, so make it easy for them by being specific in your questions. Open-ended questions can be confusing. If your contact is confused during the conversation, it becomes hard for your contact to offer help. Here are some examples of language to use and language to avoid:

Language to Use	Language to Avoid
"I have some questions about your work in relation to my skills and interests." [Name skills and interests.]	"I'd like to pick your brain."
"This is what I *like to do* and what I *think I'm good at.*"	"I don't know what I want to do."
"During my internship I would like to continue to build up some of my skills." [Name skills here.]	"What do you think I should do?"
"Can you tell me anything about the company's culture?"	"I hear it's a terrible company."

Ending a Networking Meeting and Follow-Up Actions

As you continue to network, your conversations become easier and then become second nature. But as you are talking and exploring, don't forget to ask for "the next action." You don't want to get sucked into the whirling vortex of networking—the place where you meet lots of people but see no action.

Always leave a networking meeting, asking for one or more of the following:

- An introduction to a person or an organization
- A contact to whom you should send a resume
- A resource to help you in your search
- A follow-up call if you have additional questions

You can't know if someone can or will help you until you ask. If not able to grant your specific request, that person will likely offer you information to support your search. Here are four things to do to make sure that your meeting was time well spent:

1. *At the end of your meeting,* make sure that you *repeat your "ask."*
2. *Set a day and time for follow-up.* Ensure that everyone understands the next steps.
3. **Always *end with* "Thank you for your time, help, and advice."**
4. *Send a thank you note.* After all, the people have given their time and have agreed to help you in your search.

A note about notes: E-mail thank you notes are what're expected. A pleasant surprise is a handwritten note. Either way, send your thank you note within 24 hours of meeting. If sending a handwritten note. buy notecards now, and don't forget the snail mail stamps.

Here's a Thank You Note Template

Dear [XX],

Thank you for spending time with me on [day] and for your advice as I look for an internship. I appreciate your offer of [help/ an introduction/a referral] with [XX] [company or person].

I will follow up with you on [day or date] and let you know my progress with [XX].

Thank you again for your help. I am very grateful.

Sincerely, [You]

Then, make sure you:

- Do what you say you're going to do.
- Follow up in a timely manner.
- Act quickly on the connection or advice given.

Don't Forget to Check Your Voicemail

Chances are your contact will follow up by phone or e-mail, maybe by text. Make sure there is room on your voicemail and that your message sounds professional and businesslike. "Yo! Leave it at the beep" or "Please leave a message along with your credit card number and I will return your call when I'm done shopping" is not what you want your networking contact to hear.

This Really Happened—A Cautionary Tale

Free booze!

After a full day of "informal" networking with potential employers at a financial services company, Paula and Zander were surprised to be invited, along with 10 other potential interns, to a Happy Hour event in the corporate cafeteria with managers they had shadowed during the day. Certainly, that was a good sign that the executives liked the group!

Upon arrival, they were greeted by a full bar and a bartender mixing martinis, mojitos, and margaritas. Wow! The managers headed for the mojitos, and most of the group, including Zander, followed. Paula went to the full bar and ordered a soda. There was lot of friendly talk about student activities, sports, and vacations. Since Zander was having a ball at the bar and hitting it off with a senior VP of Acquisitions, he said "Yes" to a second mojito. After all, the manager was drinking, so why shouldn't he? Paula stuck with soda, spending her time introducing herself to managers from different departments.

The evening ended. The next day, Paula got a call with an offer to interview for a specific internship. Zander did not. Surprised, Zander called the senior VP of Acquisitions to ask if he could expect an offer. The answer: "You're just 'not a good fit' for our company's culture."

Even more upset now, Zander called around to the other interns. He discovered that any candidate who was drinking alcohol at the gathering hadn't been extended an offer. The Happy Hour event turned out to be an interview filter for the firm.

Think about your response to this make-or-break moment:

Question: "I am going for a refill. What are you drinking?"
Answer: "Thanks. I appreciate it. I'll have a club soda with lime."

Down and Dirty Recap

- Create a prioritized networking list including friends, family, guidance counselors, and advisors.
- Build your executive presence by practicing what you want to say in advance and maintaining good eye contact.
- If you can, meet in person with your network contact—it's great practice for the interview.
- Learn about where your contact works. Practice conversation starters and questions.
- Be flexible and explore lots of opportunities.
- Follow up in a timely manner.
- Always ask for the next action.
- Send a handwritten thank you note.

The impression you leave now matters.

Be clear. Be concise. Be grateful.
Say "Thank you" a lot.

Today's networking conversations can easily become tomorrow's interviews.

What I Know Now (Notes)

What I Need to Do Next (Notes)

CHAPTER 6

It's Showtime!

With the advice and help from your network and the submission of a solid resume, you've gotten an interview!

Just about anything can happen when you show up for an interview. That's why this is the longest chapter in the book. It contains a lot of information to help you understand, prepare for, and perform well during an interview's inevitable make-or-break moments. Even though it's a lot to read, I promise that it will be worth your time.

What You'll Get From This Chapter

There is always lot of competition for internships. How you prepare before, act during, and follow up after your interview all form the impression you'll leave with the interviewer. The right impression puts you into the next round of interviews or gets you an offer.

This chapter will help you make a great impression and decide if the opportunity is right for you. We'll also cover the following:

- ✓ Looking and acting confident
- ✓ Asking the questions that will set you apart
- ✓ Ending your interview with an action
- ✓ Talking about compensation without fear
- ✓ Accepting or declining a position with style

Congratulations! Here's what you've learned in Chapters 1 through 5:

You're now self-aware.

You know your strengths.

You know your weaknesses—and you have plans to address them.

You have your supporting stories that demonstrate learning and employer value. Your goal is solid.

Your resume is written.

Your narrative has been road-tested with your network. Your network has helped direct you.

And now, you have an interview.

Expectations are high all around! It's time to bring it all together.

The good news is that you've already done a lot of interview practice in your networking meetings. However, interviews differ from networking conversations in three ways:

1. There is a specific position being discussed.
2. The interview takes place in a formal setting.
3. There will likely be a compensation discussion.

Time to Walk Your Resume Talk

The first thing to know about interviewers is that they are very, very intuitive people. Within the first few minutes after greeting you, a professional interviewer may not know if he or she will hire you, but the professional interviewer almost always knows if he or she won't hire you. That's why interviewers want to see you either in person or onscreen. They want to make sure you can walk your resume talk.

It takes only a few minutes for an interviewer to discover if the Paper You connects to the In-Person You. If they don't connect, you may not get hired. Think about it—your resume, and/or positive feedback from your network, got you the interview because you looked qualified, well rounded, and confident. That's the person the interviewer expects to meet.

But sometimes, in person, nerves and lack of confidence can get in the way of putting your best foot forward. With a little preparation, you can be the confident you from your resume.

Verbal Disaster Words

Talking your resume begins with how you actually speak. Remember, you are sitting across from a professional listener. You therefore must start to listen to the actual words that come out of your mouth.

The truth is we don't really listen to how we speak. Some of you reading this book may not even be aware that you probably use these **verbal disaster words** *all the time.* During make-or-break moments, these are the words that decrease your chances of getting hired:

Um
Like
Ya know

These disaster words add nothing to a conversation, and definitely make you sound unsure of yourself. Trust me: People in positions of authority (supervisors, interviewers, teachers, and others) have *no patience* for conversations that include these words. If the listener has to find your brilliant ideas in a sea of meaningless "ums," "likes," and "ya knows," you have almost certainly taken yourself out of the running.

Your Job #1 is to unlearn using these verbal disaster words. Reread your resume. Is there one "um," "like," or "ya know" anywhere? The answer is no.

The best way to take these words out of your vocabulary is to *practice listening to what you and those around you are actually saying.* It may sound weird but record a few conversations on your phone and *listen* to yourself and your friends.

Count the "ums," "likes," and "ya knows" in the first five minutes. Be prepared. When you start listening, you may not be happy with how you sound. *Changing the way you speak takes time, so start now.* It's challenging because most of the people around you are still using these words.

If you can get these words out of your everyday conversation, you will make a better first impression and you will *definitely* set yourself apart from your competition. Unlearning the verbal disaster words is a tactical advantage you can create for yourself.

Be strong! You can do it.

Spoiler Alert: You may think this doesn't apply to you because you are set to graduate with a 4.0 GPA from a top school and want to intern at a small, hip startup where "everyone talks like me." *Wrong!* Here's why.

Today you might be looking for an internship, but at some point in the future, you'll be in a job with a lot of responsibility. Let's say you love the startup culture. The reality is that every startup needs funding. Funding comes from people in positions of power and authority. Funders require clarity and confidence. The startups that get funded have articulate, confident leaders who can clearly speak about their company's goals and objectives with informed experts and investors. If your language fails to convince a funder, your idea won't get funded and it will fail. If you want to hear and see what this looks like, watch an episode of *Shark Tank*.

Working to change how you speak now is the *single most important thing* you can do to prepare for your interview later and set yourself apart as you begin your career.

Onscreen Interviews: What to Remember

- *Set up properly.* Make sure you're at a desk in a well-lit, quiet room. Check the lighting and background noise to limit distractions. Use headphones or earbuds. If you don't have a space at home that works, reserve a room at the local library.
- *Nonverbal cues.* Practice your eye contact so that you are looking at the camera on you as you are speaking. Limit fidgeting with your upper body. Be aware of how quickly you are speaking. Most of us speak faster when we're nervous.

Take notes. It can be hard to remember every detail in an interview. Either in a new screen or on paper, jot down details you want to remember or questions you want to ask or answer more thoroughly. Explain that you will be taking a few notes during the conversation, but please don't use note-taking as a crutch. Only capture essential details you can use in follow-up conversations.

In-Person Interviews: Take These to Your Interview

As you get ready to go to your interview, here are things you don't want to forget:

- *Personal business cards.* If you don't already have one, look at either Moo or Vistaprint for templates. You can also create a QR code business card on your laptop. Include your name, e-mail address, mobile number, personal website (if you have one), and a descriptor (i.e., Business Major Interested in Sports and Marketing. Graduation Date: [XX]).
- *Copies of your resume.* Even if your resume was submitted online, bring extra copies. These should be on high-quality paper. Bring five more copies than you think you'll need. More often than not, someone unexpected will "drop in" to see how you react to changes on the fly—and you'll often be interviewing with busy professionals whose schedules move around.
- *A notebook for taking notes.* Taking notes on your phone is *not* acceptable.
- *ID for getting through security.*

This Really Happened

Alima, a very accomplished young woman, was scheduled for four back-to-back interviews at the headquarters of a Fortune 50 company. She flew to the city the day before. She brought extra copies of her resume and newly printed business cards. Alima had rehearsed answers to questions about her background, and she was prepared with specific questions for each interviewer.

She had done her homework and was ready and excited. On to the interview! To reduce travel stress, Alima even got to the offices early and waited until just before her interview to sign in. Unfortunately, she left her photo ID at the hotel.

And in this security-conscious world, without the necessary ID, Alima had no chance of getting into the building. She called her contact in HR. But without an ID, her contact couldn't overrule security. By now, she had already missed the first interview. Her other interviews were canceled.

Alima took a summer job waitressing at TGI Fridays. It was a good way to make some money, but it wasn't the first step Alima wanted on her career path.

Yep, it really happened.

Follow the checklist earlier, and *don't forget your ID!*

Whoo-hoo! It's Interview Day!

Now That You've Gotten to the Interview,
Here's What to Do and Not Do

In this section, we'll focus on one thing: how to rock the interview and set yourself apart from your competition.

There's More Than One Type of Interview

Interview processes begin with a 30-minute screening. The most typical is with a Human Resources (HR) representative or through an online portal.

Online: More and more companies are using online interview platforms to create efficiency in their hiring processes. The benefit for the candidate is that they can complete the interview at their convenience within a set number of days. If you get a link to an online interviewing platform, research the platform before you do the interview, so you are familiar with its mechanics. Most online services offer sample interviews. The sample interviews walk you through their process and let you know how long you have to answer each question. Expect the questions to be straightforward. You can prepare in advance for these questions:

Why do you want to intern here?
Tell us about your strengths.
Tell us about your weaknesses.
Tell us about a time you worked in a group or collaborative setting.

The screening interview is assessing both hard skills like analysis or working with spreadsheets and softer skills like how you communicate, solve problems, and work within a team. In other words, the Big Six.

Relax and let your personality shine through!

In person: The HR representative will typically talk about the company; explain the structure of the internship; ask you about your experience, strengths, and weaknesses; ask you why you are interested in the company; and if you have any questions.

After a successful screening, one of the three things will happen: an offer, a pass-along interview, or a rejection. Here we'll talk about the pass-along interview. If the company works in an office, this will almost always be in person. You will likely tour the office and meet staff. Pay attention to what you see. Do people seem happy? Are they collaborating? What is the office vibe? Paying attention to your surroundings and answering these questions will help you decide if this is a good place to intern.

If the company is fully remote, you'll do the same "tour" online. Ask yourself the questions aforementioned and observe the team dynamic.

In all cases, be professional and let your personality shine through.

As you meet people, it's OK to write down their names and positions. After all, a lot of information will be coming at you at once and the people you meet will *not* be wearing nametags! Writing down names and titles also helps you organize thank you notes.

For technical positions in finance or engineering, you may also encounter a **problem-solving interview**. In addition to a discussion about the company and position, you will be asked how you would tackle a real or simulated problem. You may even be asked to give a short presentation. The "right answer" is less important than your thought process. The interviewer is looking to hear how you break down an issue, think, and problem solve under pressure.

Regardless of the format, make sure to have built in enough time in your schedule. You don't want to cut the interview short because you have another appointment.

Five Tips and Advice to Set Yourself Apart From Your Competition

Tip #1: Create value for your employer. We said in the beginning that internships serve two purposes: helping you take the first step in your career and helping your employer achieve business objectives. You can assume that upping your learning curve or achieving personal growth is a benefit, but not an employer's primary objective. This is why it's critical to actively connect what you've done and your goals with how you can help the company achieve its goals. Here are a few examples:

- If you have design skills, connect your experience to help with sales pitches, presentations, or updating materials.
- If you're certified in Excel, offer to teach Excel's finer points to staff.
- If you're a math major, offer help with analytics and sorting data.
- If you're a varsity athlete, offer to organize a department's sports outing.

There is *always a connection* between what you have done and what can be useful for a company. *It is up to you to connect those dots* in the interview and make it easy for an interviewer to see you as a valuable resource and strong candidate.

Tip #2: Interviews happen in real time. If you are anxious about the interview process, visualizing the experience from start to finish will help. Think about what is likely to happen, the questions you'll ask, and the answers you will give. Set up practice interviews, including video screenings, with your network or Career Services Department and take online platform interviews. Practice your body language and eye contact. Practice your answers to the most likely questions:

- Why do you want to work here?
- What have been your biggest successes and challenges so far?
- How have you applied lessons learned?

***Tip #3: Make a great* first impression *and* last impression.** What you say *first* and what you say *last* are the things that the interviewer is most likely to remember.

First impression: Your interviewer will form an impression of you within the first 30 seconds of meeting. Nail your opening! If in person, practice your handshake. It should be firm without crushing the other person's hand. Always maintain good eye contact. Begin the conversation by saying how excited you are about the opportunity.

Last impression: Equally important is how you end the conversation. In person, end with another solid handshake and with good eye contact. For in person and virtual interviews, be prepared with a clear wrap-up, next steps, and a question about the expected timeline for notification.

Don't forget to *thank the interviewer for his or her time*. Forgetting to thank the interviewer is a common oversight when interviewees are nervous.

Tip #4: You had me at "HELLO." Here's an easy acronym to keep in mind when you interview, when you network, and when you have *any* business-related conversation:

H—Handshake*
E—Eye contact
L—Listen
L—Language
O—Observation

*A virtual handshake is "Nice to see you. How has your week been so far?"

Tip #5: Be sure to follow the Top 10 Interview Dos and Don'ts (with lots of details).

Top 10 Interview Dos and Don'ts

Do	Don't
Be yourself.	Show up unprepared.
Arrive early. Dress well.	Show nervous body language.
Listen to each question. Take a breath before answering.	Rush to answer.
Be clear and concise.	Be negative.
Maintain good eye contact (which is not the same as staring).	Be distracted by your phone.
Say "I don't know" if you don't know.	Make excuses.
Tell stories.	Forget to ask about compensation.
Ask questions about responsibilities and corporate culture.	Appear desperate.
Be clear on next steps.	Treat the interview as informational.
Send a thank you note.	Forget that the interview isn't over until you leave the building.

Details: The Dos

1. *Be yourself.* An interview is a conversation between two people; even if you are answering onscreen prompts. Let your personality shine through! Interviewers are interviewing *you*, not a manufactured version of you. Present a balanced picture of yourself and always be ready to talk about strengths, weaknesses, goals, and what you can offer the organization.

   Be sure to do the following:

   - *Be truthful.* Don't overstate your experience. Interviewers *know* when you're exaggerating.
   - *Connect.* If you see a personal item in the office (vacation photo, pet photo, competition medal, etc.) and you have a similar interest, ask about it. "I noticed the photo of your dog. I grew up with a Labrador. He was the best dog ever." If interviewing virtually, find common ground by talking about hobbies, interests, and vacations.
   - *Own all of you.* We all have flaws. It's OK to talk about them within the context of how you want to grow and

improve. This will signal to the interviewer that you are humble, teachable, and self-aware—all Big Six characteristics interviewers look for in candidates.

2. *Arrive early. Dress well (in person and online).*

Arrive early. Arriving early gives you time to regroup, visit the restroom, and think about what you are going to say. If in person, allow extra time to account for traffic or a mass transit slowdown. You don't need to arrive for an interview stressed out.

Arriving early signals to the hiring manager that you are serious about the position and the interview. And if you get to an in person interview much too early, take a short walk around the block. It will help calm your nerves.

Arriving to an In-Person Interview Stress-Free

Don't rely on Google Maps. If you can, do a practice run and see how long it takes to get to your destination with traffic. Build in an extra 30 minutes to account for traffic, unforeseen accidents and construction delays, and a coffee or pit stop.

Chatting with the receptionist. Receptionists are the gatekeepers of the office. They know a lot more than the location of the closet and the restroom. Introduce yourself and ask the receptionist his or her name. If the receptionist seems open to it, ask the receptionist a question about the company that involves a timely topic, perhaps something you heard or read on your news feed. This kind of conversation is also a great way to relax and warm up.

After your interview, your interviewer is likely to walk you out to the receptionist's area. The interviewer will notice that you are saying good-bye to the receptionist by name. And if you call back with a follow-up question or to reach someone else in the organization, the receptionist, remembering you, can direct you to the best person for help.

Don't wait in the reception area glued to your phone. Look around, and see who is coming in and going out. Notice how people are dressed. Do they seem happy? You can learn a lot from observing a company from the reception area.

Dress well. We said at the beginning that interviewers will often decide on your candidacy in the first few minutes of meeting you. How you dress is part of that decision. Even if you think you are interviewing with a "casual" company, casually dressing for an interview says that you are not taking the process seriously. Once you become an intern, you can dress like the rest of the people in the office.

Guidelines for Dressing Appropriately (In-Person and Virtual)

- Dress respectfully, one step up from what you see in or believe about the office.
- Don't wear low-cut shirts or short skirts.
- Be clean. Make sure that your clothes are pressed and have no visible stains.
- Wear dress shoes or flat shoes. No sneakers or stilettos.
- Show off your personality in a business-appropriate way. If you wear a gray suit, spice up your look with a patterned shirt or cool socks.
- For corporate interviews, tone down your jewelry.
- Cover your body art. You want the interviewer to focus on what you're saying, not your body art.
- Wear daytime makeup, not nighttime going-out makeup.

3. *Listen to each question. Take a breath before answering.* Here are typical questions that interviewers ask. You can think about and prepare your answers in advance.
    1. What are your strengths and weaknesses?
        - Talk about how you overcame or are working on a weakness without being negative.
    2. What are your goals for this internship?
    3. Explain a personal success or failure.
        - Focus on what you learned and how you applied the lesson.
    4. What classes do you like the most, and what classes do you like the least?
    5. Why did you pick your major?
    6. Why do you want to work here?

7. What are your goals after graduation?

8. Where do you see yourself fitting into this organization?
   - Research the company so you know how it operates.

9. How well do you work in collaborative situations or groups?
   - Have examples ready.

10. Talk about your past employment.
    - Tell the interviewer what you liked, didn't like, and learned.

11. What's the most creative thing you've done?

12. What's something you're proud of?

Trick Questions

Sometimes, but rarely for internships, interviewers throw a question at a candidate that seems out of left field. An interviewer may ask, "Why are light bulbs round?" or "How many Venti coffees did Starbucks sell last year?" These questions are not about what you know; they are about what and how you think. These questions are asked to see how you react to the unexpected in real time. If you do get one of these questions, *relax*. Answer with a sense of humor and maybe even a personal story.

Example

Interviewer question: "How many Venti coffees did Starbucks sell last year?" Your Answer: "I don't know, but they sold over 50 to me alone. I bet that information is in the Starbucks annual report." Then you can follow up with your own questions and a bit of humor, for example, "Are you a Starbucks or Dunkin' person?"

This Really Happened

On a rainy Friday, Lewis was interviewing for an internship at a small, privately held, service-oriented company. Because CEOs are very visible in small companies, the CEO dropped by the interview to introduce himself. Lewis, the interviewer, and the CEO chatted for a few minutes.

As the CEO was leaving, he turned and asked Lewis if, after his interview, he wouldn't mind helping move a large IKEA box from his car into the building. It was raining hard that day, and Lewis was wearing a suit. Lewis's in-the-moment answer:

I'd love to. As a matter of fact, I just helped my girlfriend put together some IKEA furniture and got good at following those picture directions. After we get the box inside, I'd be happy to help you put it together.

Lewis had in fact helped his girlfriend the weekend before. However, it turned out that there was no IKEA box in the CEO's car. It was the CEO's way to gauge Lewis's reaction to pitching in on menial tasks.

Lewis was offered the position—because he was prepared, relaxed, and flexible in the interview. ***You won't be able to plan for a trick question, so just be yourself.***

4. *Be clear and concise.* Practice answers to the interview questions in Tip #3. If you don't understand a question, ask the interviewer to *please* repeat or rephrase what he or she said. *Always answer the question being asked.* If you don't, you'll sound like a politician. Since an interview is a conversation, feel free to follow up with a question of your own.

5. *Maintain good eye contact.* I can't say enough about this. Eyes are the windows to the soul—really. Eye contact is a nonverbal indicator of confidence. Good eye contact builds immediate trust. Even if you feel confident, bad eye contact communicates lack of confidence, an impression you don't want to leave. Here are some things about eye contact to remember:

   • Not looking at the interviewer signals that you are unsure of your answer.
   • Staring at the interviewer is off-putting and just plain creepy. Please blink.
   • Looking up and to the left is associated with "I don't know."
   • Looking up and to the right is often interpreted as not telling the truth.

- Looking up can also be interpreted as an "eye roll" and a sign of boredom.
- Looking down indicates submission or feeling guilty.
- Looking down can also be interpreted as not being prepared.

   How to practice: Practice on your pets; siblings; and conversations with friends, teachers, adults, people in the grocery store or coffee shop, or anywhere else you talk to people. Pets crave affection and will keep your eye contact. Siblings might look away, just like an interviewer, but that, too, is great practice. Adults will appreciate being part of the exercise. Networking meetings are also a great opportunity to practice good eye contact.

6. *Say "I don't know" if you don't know.* This is part of "Be yourself." If you don't know something, don't make up an answer. After all, you are getting an internship to learn, so of course you don't know everything! *Own it* and say, "I don't know, but I'm going to find out and get back to you tomorrow." This is a great opportunity to stay in touch. After the interview, find out what you agreed to research and include it in your follow-up e-mail.

   Here's how you address the unanswered question in your follow-up e-mail: "You asked a great question during our conversation about [X]. I didn't have the answer then, but I was curious, and this is what I've learned." Your enthusiastic follow-up to an "I don't know" moment shows more Big Six traits: teach-ability, humility, and problem-solving skills.

7. *Tell stories.* People rarely forget facts, but they always remember how you made them feel. And they remember stories. Take another look at your resume and think about any stories you can add. You may not use them all, but you'll be prepared.

   Here's a reminder of what a memorable story includes:
   - Challenge
   - Solution
   - Outcome
   - Lessons learned
   - How you've applied the learning

8. *Ask questions about responsibilities and corporate culture.* First, a comment on the importance of "reading the room." Understanding how

your interviewer is approaching the interview will help you choose the best questions to ask and stories to tell.

✓ Listen carefully to the interviewer's tone of voice and wording of questions.
✓ Does the interviewer seem distracted or enthusiastic?
✓ Are you being asked "formula questions"?
✓ Did the interviewer take the time to read your resume and customize the questions to your experience and skills?

Interviewers are people too, and anyone can have a bad day. If your interviewer is distracted and asking formula questions, try to shift the conversation to insert your most memorable stories that highlight your skills and experience. In these instances, you will have to work a bit harder to stand out and set yourself apart.

When you are asking questions about roles and responsibilities, be specific. You want to get the information you need to figure out if the internship will be fun, challenging, and rewarding—a "good fit." Here are examples of questions to ask:

• How many years has the company had interns and an internship program?
• How is the internship program organized?
• What is the company's goal for the internship program?
• What are the long-term goals of the company?
• Is the company in a growth mode?
• I read about the company values on the website. I was especially interested in [X]. Can you tell me more about the company culture?
• How is the department I will be working in growing or changing?
• What academic classes have helped past interns succeed?
• What are the overall expectations for an intern?
• What are the typical responsibilities of an intern in [X] department?
• Does the intern work address existing client needs or issues, new business development, or something else?

- What is a typical day for an intern?
- Can you tell me more about past interns and what has worked well and not well for them?
- [If there is an intern project] Can you talk a bit about how the intern project is structured?
  - How many interns typically work on a project?
  - If the project is a presentation, how is it handled: with one presenter or group presentation?
  - What is the timeline for the internship project?
  - What are the resources interns can use to complete the project?
  - How many interns are in the group?
- Do interns have mentors?
- Do interns collaborate with other departments? If so, what is the process for collaborating and getting information?
- Is there an opportunity to socialize with staff outside of work such as at a company picnic, at staff outings, or in softball leagues?
- I also have a goal for the internship. My goal is [XX]. How can working toward this fit into the intern program?
- Are interns ever offered full-time employment after graduation?
- If interns are offered full-time employment, how many or what percentage of interns typically accept?

These questions will give you the information you need to understand more about the company, how the department works, and how interns are expected to contribute.

Talking, Listening, and Answering

The question of how much talking to do in an interview comes up all the time. Don't hog the time. Your goal for the interview is to spend 40 percent of the time telling your story and 60 percent of the time gathering information. This is why it's important to be clear and concise when you talk about yourself.

More information = Ability to make the right decision for you

9. *Be clear on next steps.* At the end of your interview, ask about next steps. Here are some "next step" questions to ask:
   - Is there anything I should know that I haven't asked?
   - When do you anticipate making a hiring decision?
   - How will candidates be notified?
   - When is the most convenient time to follow up?
   - Can I expect a team interview or a technical interview [if it is for a technical position]?
   - If I make it to the next round, will it involve a project or development of a presentation?

   Always leave the interview with a game plan!

   Finally, if you want the internship, then ask for it! Tell the interviewer that this is your first choice and what you like most about the opportunity and the company. Interviewers want to make offers to those who are enthusiastic, are focused, and will accept.

10. *Send a thank you note.* Most interviewers appreciate an e-mailed thank you note. Interviewers see a lot of people, so stand out with your thank you note by reminding the interviewer of who you are and talking about specific details and connections made in your meeting. Mention that you learned a lot and thank the interviewer for his or her time. If you had a panel interview, send a note to each member of the panel containing, wherever possible, specific details about your conversation. Send your note within 24 hours of the interview. If you write a handwritten note and you have time, drop off the note(s) to your new friend, the receptionist.

If you have follow-up questions or answers to something that came up in the interview, e-mail is the best way to communicate.

Details: The Don'ts

1. *Don't show up unprepared.* Research the company. Read through its website, press releases, and annual reports. Understand its mission

and values, and learn what you can about the culture. Google the company to find out if it's been in the news. Ask questions in your interview about recent press coverage. This is all public record stuff, so use it.

2. *Don't show nervous body language.* It's OK to feel nervous, that's natural, but nervousness becomes negative when it becomes a distraction. When you get nervous, do you:
   - Squirm in your chair?
   - Constantly change position?
   - Tap your foot?
   - Click a pen?
   - Play with your hair (including tucking your hair behind your ears)?
   - Bite your nails?
   - Touch your face?
   - Wave your arms while you're talking?
   - Laugh nervously?

   You may not realize you're doing these things. These are habits picked up over time. The only way you'll know before the interview if you have these habits is to ask someone to observe your behavior and tell you if you demonstrate any of these habits. Be brave.

   Have one or two practice interviews with a trusted advisor or someone in your network. Ask for specific feedback about your body language so you can become aware of what you are doing. Then, correct the behavior.

   Interviewers pick up instantly on nervous behavior. These habits are a big, negative factor in the impression you'll leave.

3. *Don't rush to answer.* If you are nervous, you might have a tendency to jump in, cut off, or talk over the interviewer. This signals that you're not really listening. Calm your nerves through controlled breathing. When the interviewer is talking, don't hold your breath! Focus on breathing in and out. Holding your breath is more common than you may think and makes nervousness worse.

4. *Don't be negative.* Ever heard the saying "Bad news travels 10 times faster than good news"? Sometimes when we're nervous, we focus on a negative experience to highlight a point. Examples of this are

"My last summer job was very boring" and "Last year, I really didn't like my boss." These may be true. Part of preparing for the interview is to get beyond what you *thought* of the experience and talk about what you *learned from it*—and how it could apply to the current position. Focus on learning and growth rather than on problems and frustrations. Definitely practice these explanations in advance.

The impression you want to leave is that despite challenges and less-than-ideal circumstances, you remained positive. Leave the interviewer feeling that you're open to new suggestions, open to new learning, and willing to listen. In other words, come across as teachable and adaptable.

5. *Don't be distracted by your phone.* Your phone is a major distraction. If you take your phone to an interview—virtual or in person—turn it off and *put it in the* bottom *of your bag* so you won't be tempted by it. If you don't have a bag, put it in inside your jacket pocket. Don't be tempted to look at your phone in the reception area. Use that time to observe and form your impression of the company.

6. *Don't make excuses.* Employers value a person's willingness to own the person's actions. If you are late to the interview, if you're not prepared, or if you're completely stumped by a question, own it! Be humble and honest. And if you don't know something, speak up and ask!

7. *Don't forget to ask about compensation.* Once you have enough information about the company, position, and "fit" *and* you are interested in the internship, then it's time to ask about compensation. Many people are uncomfortable talking about money. Get used to it. This is a conversation you will have throughout your career, so you might as well start now.

If it's a paid position, it's usually listed in the description. If the compensation isn't clear, do some research. Ask your Career Services Department for help, and/or track down former interns (try LinkedIn) and ask them about their experience as a whole and about compensation.

If you still can't find an answer, don't be afraid to ask your interviewer. Save the question for *the end of your discussion*. Frame your question like this: "It wasn't clear from the job description if a stipend or compensation accompanies the internship. Can you clarify this for me?" Be prepared with a response to "No, this position is not compensated. Does this affect your interest level?"

Practice your response (yes or no) to the earlier question, and make sure your eye contact and tone of voice remain positive. When compensation is not offered, ask if the company reimburses for transportation or lunch so you are incurring minimal expense.

What to do if you are not able to accept an unpaid internship: If you are interested in the company and the position but cannot consider an unpaid internship, prepare for an honest conversation with the interviewer. Start by asking the interviewer for advice.

It may be possible for the employer to shorten the internship to two to three days per week, so you can supplement your internship with a part-time paying job. It's possible the company could hire you as a freelance contractor. Chances are your employer has been down this road before. If the employer likes you and wants you as an intern, then the employer will do whatever is possible to make the position work.

8. *Don't appear desperate.* Use these ways to avoid a desperate search:
   - *Start looking early.* The best positions are filled early. If you are looking in the financial services industry, most intern positions are filled in October, seven months before they begin. If you are interested in financial services or tech sector, start your search the prior January (12 to 18 months in advance).
   - *Research and apply for* at least three *different positions.* You will expand the likelihood of multiple offers, get more interview practice, and decrease the chances of looking desperate during any one interview.
   - *Have a fallback.* If no internships work out, think about where else you can work and get relevant experience.

If you've started your search early and have come up short, you will still be ahead of most summer job applicants.

- *Get creative.* If a five-day-per-week internship is not working out for you, can you piece together a two-day-per-week unpaid internship with a three-day-per-week paying summer job? *There is always more than one way to get the result you want.* This demonstrates adaptability and problem solving and will give you great stories for next year's interviews.

9. *Don't treat the interview as informational.* Internship interviews are for positions. Informational interviews are for *information,* but many have resulted in internship offers. The lesson here is to treat *every* interview as a position interview.

To clarify, the purpose of an informational interview is to learn more about the company and its culture as well as to make connections. Informational interviews happen when there is no open position. You can have informational interviews as far as a year in advance of your internship search. Going on an informational interview is a great way to build your network and relationships within the company in advance of an open position.

Be as prepared for an informational interview as you would be for a position interview. Research the company and have questions and stories ready, just as you would for an interview for an open internship position. Set up short, informational interviews with your LinkedIn connections. It's never too early to connect with people who work at your target companies.

Today's interviewers are tomorrow's networking contacts.

Any conversation, whether informational or for a position, builds your network. If you are interviewing for a position and like the company but are not offered an internship, stay in touch with everyone you've met. People know people, and now that they know *you,* they can make introductions on your behalf. Here is a spreadsheet similar to the one you created for managing your network that will keep you organized for future opportunities. Don't forget to connect with everyone you meet on LinkedIn.

Network Everywhere Chart

Contact	
Company	
Meeting Date	
Subjects Discussed	
Date: Follow-Up #1	
Subjects: Follow-Up #1	
Date: Follow-Up #2	
Subjects: Follow-Up #2	

Having this information in one place makes it easier to stay motivated, keep your follow-up promises, and establish yourself as trustworthy, motivated, and enthusiastic.

10. *In person—Don't forget that the interview isn't over until you leave the building.* Until you are in your car or on the bus, train, or subway, the interview is *not over.* As you leave your interview, make a point of saying goodbye to your new pal—the receptionist. While you're waiting for the elevator or on the ride down, there's a good chance that you'll meet someone from the company. This is a good opportunity to introduce yourself and to have a short conversation. Ask the person what he or she does and likes most about the company. Mention that you have just interviewed for an internship position. If you are paying attention and proactive, this is what *could* and *did* happen.

This Really Happened

The scene: Maura and another person are waiting for the elevator after your interview.

| MAURA: | Hi. Do you work here? |
| OTHER PERSON: | Yes, I do. |

MAURA: I just interviewed for an internship. May I ask what do you do for the company?

OTHER PERSON: I am the CEO, Steve Brown. Nice to meet you. [*CEOs take the elevator too!*]

MAURA: Nice to meet you. I'm Maura Sharif. I just had a great conversation with Jamel in HR. I'm very interested in an internship here.

OTHER PERSON: I am glad to hear that.

MAURA: Here is my business card. This is definitely my first choice for an internship.

OTHER PERSON: Thanks, Maura. Best of luck to you.

MAURA: Thanks, Mr. Brown. I look forward to staying in touch.

The elevator door opens.

This exchange took 10 seconds, but look at what happened! Maura met and gave her business card to the CEO, while setting the stage for a follow-up conversation. But this conversation will never happen if you are in an elevator staring at your phone, wearing earbuds, or changing your shoes. The opportunity will slip by—and you'll never even know it was there. As Wayne Gretzky, one of the best hockey players of all time, said, "You miss 100 percent of the shots you don't take."

And if all goes well, the next thing you'll hear is "Congratulations! We're excited to offer you an internship."

Here's how to accept the position with style and gratitude:

What to Do	What to Say
Thank the interviewer.	"I am flattered and excited about the offer. This was my first choice for an internship."
Get the facts.	"Can we review [start date, responsibilities, other interns, compensation, company holidays]…?"
Understand the timeline.	"I read that the orientation date is [X]. Is that still correct?"
Reconfirm compensation.	"I understand that the total [or weekly] compensation is [X]."
Ask if you can reach out to the staff.	"I am very excited to start. Is it appropriate to reach out to the team?"

What to Do	What to Say
Ask for additional details.	"Is there anything else that we didn't cover that I should know?"
Thank the interviewer again.	"Thank you again. I am very excited." (If it's an in-person offer, give a firm handshake and make good eye contact.)
Send a thank you note to all relevant parties.	Within 24 hours, send a note and include the following: • "I enjoyed meeting everyone." • Mention of specific detail(s) about the process. • "I am looking forward to getting started."

Accepting an internship offer should make you feel happy. If it doesn't, the internship isn't right. It's OK to decline an offer if it's done in a timely manner and leaves the door open for future conversations. What you want to avoid is people thinking that you've wasted their time. That is a negative last impression that can follow you when looking for future jobs. Keep the door open; an internship is only the first step in your career!

So Now, the Flip Side: What If You're Offered a Position and Need More Time or Plan to Decline the Offer?

Whatever your ultimate decision, the most important thing is to leave a positive last impression and an "open door" for future opportunities. There is a **right to stay in touch with these new contacts you have met along the way.** You may be interested in the company in the future, so stay in touch with everyone you've met.

What to Do	What to Say
Always begin by thanking the interviewer.	"I am flattered and excited about the offer, but…."
Be transparent if you are waiting to hear from other companies. (Prepare in advance, because you may have to make a decision in the moment.)	"As part of my interview process, I have recently interviewed with [X]. Their timeline for making a decision is [X]. What is your timeline for a decision?"
Talk about the timeline if you already have another offer.	"I have recently had another internship offer, and there is a lot to consider. Is it possible to think about the opportunity overnight [or over the weekend if it's Friday]?"

(Continues)

(*Continued*)

What to Do	What to Say
Ask for additional details.	"Is there anything we didn't cover that I should know? I am asking because I am also interviewing with other firms and want to have all of the information possible."
Get creative.	"I am flattered by the offer, but because there is no compensation, it's impossible for me to accept. I appreciate your taking the time to consider my application and talk through different options. I would very much like to stay in touch for the future."
Keep the door open.	"Thank you again for this offer. Although I must decline because of [X], I would like to stay in touch to discuss future opportunities."
Follow up	Within 24 hours, send a thank you note to everyone you met, and include the following: • "I enjoyed meeting everyone." • Mention of specific details about the process. Statement that you would like to keep in touch (and then actually keep in touch!)

This Really Happened

Nathan was a junior in college with a major in sports management. Through his network, he landed a dream interview with a minor-league baseball team. Nathan knew he nailed the interview. Before leaving the interview, HR confirmed that he would be notified of the team's decision within a week. Nathan went home, wrote his thank you note, and waited.

The week passed, and then another and another. Disappointed, Nathan took a summer job at the local smoothie shop.

One day, his phone rang, but he was serving a customer and didn't pick up the call. Later, he checked his missed calls and noticed an unopened, three-week-old voicemail. It turned out that the voicemail was from the team with an enthusiastic offer to intern. Unfortunately, Nathan missed the call and a big step toward his chosen career.

What to Do So You Won't Miss the Call

1. Confirm how the company communicates with its intern candidates. Interviewers typically notify candidates by phone or e-mail, not text messaging.

2. Before you interview for a position, make sure there is space in your voicemail. No one wants to hear, "This mailbox is full and cannot accept messages. Goodbye!"

3. If you confirm next steps and don't hear back, follow up within a reasonable amount of time, usually within 10 days to 2 weeks, with a call to the interviewer.

4. We've said this before, but here it is again: Record a work-appropriate voicemail message. "Leave it at the beep" is not what a hiring manager wants to hear.

Down and Dirty Recap

- Research and pursue more than one internship position.
- Practice answering standard and trick questions.
- Develop your own questions. Practice asking them.
- Come to the interview confident and ready.
- Nail HELLO.
- Pay attention to what you see in the office.
- Listen more; talk less.
- Practice good eye contact and positive body language.
- Don't be negative.
- Accept or decline a position the right way.
- Keep networking.
- Enjoy yourself.

When you're interviewing, everyone tells you to "be yourself." What interviewers are listening for is your "strategic self." Connect as many of your stories and facts to the Big Six as possible. Ask lots of questions. Interviews are as much about the company interviewing you as about you interviewing the company.

What I Know Now (Notes)

What I Need to Do Next (Notes)

PART 2

You're In!

Congratulations! You're an intern! Today is the first day of your business career. You are now ready to absorb all that the working world has to offer.

But First, a Pause

Before we get started with Part 2, let's fast-forward to the last day of your internship. If you can visualize what you want that day to look like, you can plan for two things: (1) how you want to act for the next 6 to 10 weeks and (2) how you want to be remembered by the people you meet.

Start by answering these three questions:

1. If you were writing a post internship recommendation of yourself, what would you want it to say?

   _____

   _____

   _____

2. What are five qualities you want people to remember *most* about you after the program ends?

   1. _____

   2. _____

   3. _____

   4. _____

   5. _____

3. What do you need to **learn** or do, or how do you need to **act** *now* to get the above results?

   Learn:

   _____

   Act:

   _____

Understanding what you want at the end makes it easier for you to plan in the beginning.

There is an overwhelming chance that you will be hired by, report to, have a department headed by, or have clients who are from the pre-Google and presmartphone generation. These people were raised on, know the value of, and reward in-person (face-to-face or video) conversations.

That's why Part 2 is about fitting in. Part 2 addresses these areas:

- How you are expected to act in the business world
- How to make a great impression
- How to form lasting relationships with the other interns and staff

We'll talk about ways in which you can improve your communication and interpersonal skills to create positive, memorable impressions. Not only will these tips and advice help you in your internship, they also help in all areas of your life.

Remember, everything that you do communicates something about you.

Here we go....

CHAPTER 7

Brutally Honest Advice About Business Behavior

What You'll Get From This Chapter

Now, you're inside. Time to live up to the expectations of the business world. Since you've never worked in this environment before, it's a little unfair for employers to even have expectations of interns—but hey, life isn't always fair.

This chapter will help you understand and exceed your employer's expectations when it comes to your behavior. We'll cover the following issues:

- ✓ Looking professional
- ✓ Making a great first impression
- ✓ Elevator etiquette
- ✓ Online etiquette
- ✓ Pro tips for remembering names

How to Put Your Best Foot Forward

Your first few days will be exciting and exhausting. You'll meet lots of new people while you learn about the company and your role as an intern. Mastering the following techniques will set you apart right from the beginning of your internship.

You've Got Three Seconds

First impressions matter, and they matter a lot.

As a species, when confronted by something or someone new, we're hardwired to react with a "fight or flight" response, the three-second window when we decide if a situation is safe or dangerous. Once we decide, we react. We're no longer running from saber-toothed tigers, but the immediate nature of responding to new situations remains in our DNA. In business, the "fight or flight" reaction is a first impression.

Think about the last time you met someone new. How long did it take you to form an impression of that person? What factors contributed to that impression?

A first impression is an immediate assessment of trustworthiness and relatability. Once formed, especially if it's a negative impression, it takes *lots* of extra work to change the perception.

What's interesting about first impressions is that they are formed largely through nonverbal communication. According to Albert Mehrabian, PhD, professor emeritus of psychology at UCLA, a first impression is based on the following:

- 55 percent nonverbal communication—facial expression, body language, appearance
- 38 percent voice quality—tone, cadence, the *way* in which words are spoken
- 7 percent words—content of what's being said

These are good things to remember if you want to make a positive first impression as the first step to being offered a full-time position, to a good recommendation, or to expand your network. So, from the start, treat every interaction with a new person in and around the office as an extension of the interview process.

What follows is advice you can use every day to help you leave a great first impression.

Your Nonverbal First Impression Indicators: Appearance and Body Language

How You Look: Fit in, but Stand Out

It may sound shallow, but how you dress in business matters. Until you learn otherwise, dress for work as you did during the interview process. Both online and in person, people will see you before they hear you. If you're not sure about the dress code, contact Human Resources the week before you begin and ask about the dress code, for the company and your department.

How You Look: Body Language and Your Connection With Your Phone

In Chapter 6, we talked about body language and eye contact within the context of an interview. Remember HELLO? Good eye contact is important for creating an immediate bond of trust and a positive first impression.

In addition to eye contact, your posture contributes to your professional image. How you physically present yourself reflects your level of confidence. Here are some examples of common body language and what you communicate with each gesture.

In person:

1. When you stand with your arms crossed in front of you, the impression you give is resistant and defensive.

2. Standing with one hand on your hip sends the message that you are bored or are skeptical of what you are hearing.

3. Putting your hands in your pockets makes others feel like you are hiding something. This posture also tends to lead to fidgeting.

4. Clasping your hands in front of you makes you look insecure.

5. Hunching over makes you look afraid.

Although it will seem uncomfortable in the beginning, practice standing up straight with equal weight on both feet and hands at your sides. It's a posture that signals receptivity to ideas and that you're open to discussion.

Online:

1. Hunching in front of the camera makes you look uncertain.
2. Keeping your camera off sends the message that you are bored and disengaged. If there is a reason why your camera needs to be off during a meeting, let your colleagues know.
3. Excessive fidgeting is a read that you are nervous.
4. Looking away from the camera often signals that you are distracted.

Body Language Activity

This may seem old school but watch newscasters on television. See how they stand, how they use their body language, and how they create eye contact. They're trained to use, but not overuse, their hands to reinforce a point they've made and to engage their audience.

Notice that they always look relaxed, approachable, and trustworthy. With a little practice, you can present yourself this way too!

Glued to Your Phone?

We love our phones.
When we have a free 10 seconds, we check them.
When we are waiting for an elevator, we check them.
When we hear a "ding," we check our phone.
When we are in the restroom, we check our phone.
A quick post. A retweet. A quick check of Instagram or Facebook.

It takes just two seconds. But while you're on your phone, you're not paying attention to what is happening around you.

The Myth of Multitasking

The "executive function" area of our brain helps us prioritize and make decisions as we move quickly from one task to another. Because our brains work quickly, it seems like we can do more than one thing at once. But the truth is **multitasking is a myth**. We are wired to do only one thing at a time. When you use your in-between time to look at your phone, you take your brain off task. The end result is that you feel stressed and anxious.

If you are on your phone, you are not really focusing on other tasks, listening to what others are saying, or observing what is happening in your environment.

Focusing, listening, and observing are the activities that will help you understand your office culture.

Executives who see you excessively on your phone interpret what they see as someone not engaged in the work or the internship. Whether this is true or not doesn't really matter. It's the *impression* you'll leave on the decision makers around you—the same people who will write your recommendation or advocate for you to become a full-time employee. Load your internal communication and social media platforms on your computer so you can detether from your phone and be present to observe what's going on around you. Even if you see executives overuse their phones, that doesn't give you permission to do the same.

Limit your personal phone time to three check-ins per day. Your friends and followers will understand.

Your Verbal First Impression Indicators: Content and Tone

How You Sound: What Other People Hear—"Um," "Like," and "Ya Know"

Chatting with your co-workers or other interns in a hallway, in an elevator, or outside an office is fun. But don't forget that in a public place like the break room or outside a cubicle, others can hear a conversation. Whether listening consciously or from down the hall, people are forming an impression of you based on what they hear. There is no faster way to make a negative first impression than by using "um," "like," or "ya know" when you are talking. Using these words makes you sound tentative, immature, and hard to follow.

Bottom line: When you use these words, you lose credibility.

Unfortunately, these words have become an ingrained part of daily speech, so much so that we don't hear them or realize we are using them. Changing this pattern of speaking is hard, but it's important.

We've talked about being aware of these words before, and here is another visual activity to do to help remove these words from your every-day language:

1. Put quarters, dimes, nickels, and pennies in a pile.
2. Ask someone you trust to take a coin every time you use "um," "like," and "ya know" in a two-minute conversation.
3. At the end of the conversation, count the coins they took.
4. Did you just give away your coffee money?
5. Use the exercise as a visual reminder to start *listening* to yourself in daily conversation.
6. Repeat the exercise every few days until you don't give away any more money.

How You Sound: Voice Modulation and Tone

Of the three elements that make up a first impression, your voice and the confidence it communicates make up almost 40 percent. Often, when we are unsure of facts or not completely comfortable in a situation, our voice rises at the end of a sentence. This signals the listener that we are feeling insecure about what we are saying. Voice modulation, especially when you are nervous, takes practice.

Here is another old school yet effective way to get good at voice modulation: First, spend 10 minutes just listening, not watching a TV or radio news report. Professional announcers are great at beginning and ending a sentence at the same vocal tone and pitch. You will notice that their voice never rises up at the end of the sentence, even when the news is bad or circumstances dramatic. Even with a modulated pitch, announcers communicate enthusiasm and excitement. You can do this too. It just takes a bit of practice.

Issues with pitch are most noticeable is when you are asking a question. Your voice doesn't need to rise up at the end of the question for your audience to know it's a question. Practice asking questions with the same tone and pitch. This will help you sound more thoughtful, credible, and professional.

Voice Modulation Activity

You can also record your voice as you read a paragraph from a newspaper article. Pay attention to what happens to your voice at the end of each sentence or question. Listen to how others speak. Once you tune in to those using even tone and pitch and "hear it," you can change the behavior for yourself.

In Person: Quick Reminder on Handshakes and Remembering Names

Believe it or not, a good handshake is memorable. Unfortunately, so is a bad handshake. This is easy to get right with just a little bit of practice and will go far in helping you create a positive first impression. Start working today on a confident handshake that doesn't crush the other person's hand!

And please, no wimpy handshakes!

Add good eye contact and a smile, and you'll be good to go.

Remembering Names

When you begin your internship, everything and almost everyone is new, and the environment can be a bit overwhelming. Unless you are fully remote with names appearing onscreen, it can be difficult to remember everyone's name. The easiest way to remember someone's name is to repeat it when you first meet the person: "Hi, Bob, it's nice to meet you."

This approach serves three purposes:

1. It affirms that you have heard the person's name.
2. It's respectful.
3. It helps you remember the name.

Mentally connect something about the person with their name. Example: Bob, brown hair. This makes that person's name easier to remember.

What to Do When You Forget a Name

We all forget names. It can be embarrassing, but it is *more* embarrassing *not* to correct the mistake in the moment. If you have met someone at the Tuesday staff meeting and see that person again on Thursday but have forgotten their name, just ask. *Do it immediately!* Don't wait. Phrase the question like this: "I know that we met on Tuesday, but I've met so many people this week, I can't remember your name. Please remind me."

After You Meet Someone, Follow Up and Connect

Within 24 hours of meeting another employee, send an e-mail and acknowledge that it was great to meet them and that you look forward to working together. Connect with that person on LinkedIn. These will be valuable future contacts when you begin to look for a full-time position.

The Elevator: Where Many First Impressions Are Formed

All employees, including your boss and the CEO, take the elevator. Elevators offer a captive audience and are a great place to meet people from your company. What that means is that your actions and behaviors in the elevator matter. Use elevator time to your advantage. Elevators are a place where many first impressions are formed.

Here's some elevator etiquette that will almost certainly help build your network.

Elevator Etiquette

Elevator Dos	Elevator Don'ts
Use the time to mentally prepare for your day	Stare at the floor or at your phone
Make general eye contact with others upon entering	Blast music through your earbuds
Smile	Chat about last night's party
Say "Hello," "good morning," or "good evening" upon entering	Change your shoes in the elevator (you can do that at your desk)
Wish others "good day" or "good evening" upon exiting	Talk in code or acronyms
Ask about how the colleague's week is going	Bring up any proprietary business or projects that the colleagues are working on

Talking in the Elevator

Crowded elevators are often quiet places. They are a space for people to reset and take a mental break. Don't chat loudly about last night's date, game, or party.

They're subjects that are interesting only to you. Other riders find it rude. The elevator is never a place to discuss work projects. You never know if a competitor or vendor is in the elevator.

However, if you find yourself in an elevator with someone you recognize from your company, try to strike up a small talk. Remind that person who you are and how you met. Ask about weekend or vacation plans. Short and sweet.

Your Secret Weapon

The most powerful nonverbal tool you have is your smile. Use it often! Smiles build trust and add to your confidence level. Interns who don't smile are perceived as nervous, bored, stressed out, or frustrated. Even if you are all these things, you don't have to show it. People respond to others who are calm, confident, and happy.

The first days of internships are exciting and will go by quickly. You'll meet other interns and staff and spend most of your time getting oriented. The first few days are also about setting expectations for the internship—what will be expected of you and what you can expect from the company. It's a great time to meet people, ask questions, and gather lots of information.

Down and Dirty Recap

- Remember that first impressions matter.
- Lose "um," "like," and "ya know."
- Practice good body language, eye contact, and voice modulation.
- Own a firm and confident handshake.
- Create associations to remember names.
- Disconnect from your phone.

What I Know Now (Notes)

What I Need to Do Next (Notes)

CHAPTER 8

Your Intern Squad

What You'll Get From This Chapter

The company chose you, and you chose the company. Now, you have to quickly figure out how to fit in with the other interns.

This chapter will help you understand how to:

- ✓ Assess the personalities around you.
- ✓ Leverage your strengths within the company.
- ✓ Use others' strengths to help you achieve your internship goal.

This last one sounds self-serving, *but it's really about collaboration.*

You already know that many companies hire interns to "road test" them for full-time employment. You were hired for, among other qualities, your perspective on business challenges. Working within a new team, communicating well, and being adaptable to new situations are three of the Big Six. How you perform in these areas as an intern point to how you will perform as an employee. Employers *are* paying attention to how you think and what you say.

Not to make you paranoid, but they're always watching.

Here you are, in a room full of intern strangers. The expectation is that you will work well together and create a work product in a relatively short time.

Business doesn't operate on academic time; it moves at the speed of markets. An internship cycle that lasts 6 to 10 weeks doesn't allow for a long, drawn-out "getting to know you" period. There will be supervision, but probably no formal rubric to follow. That means you must assess the other interns quickly and figure out how and where you can collaborate.

Pay close attention during the first few days. Despite what you may think, training isn't fluff time where you can take it easy and expect to ask someone later. It's an opportunity to be helpful to other interns (and full-time colleagues) later.

Make the most of the orientation time to learn about the other interns and figure out where you fit best within the group. Remember, one measure of success is how well you collaborate with this group of strangers.

The following three guidelines will help you succeed from the beginning of your internship and organize what you learn along the way.

Stop, Look, Listen

We've talked about how you create a first impression for others. Now it's your turn to form a first impression of the other interns. Observe the individuals and the team dynamic. Trust me, the other interns will be looking at you and doing the same.

Because you will be working together every day, as you observe, keep an open mind. If another intern has made a bad first impression, give that other intern a break. That person could just be having a bad first few days. Rather than focusing on what you don't like about the person, look for places where you can collaborate. These are areas where you can leverage your strengths and skills.

As an example, an intern may hate math but love graphic design. This person won't be too helpful with budget analysis but will be the go-to for presentation and PowerPoint design for the intern project.

As you are observing the other interns (or staff if you are the only intern), consider the following:

- Who are the extroverts?
- Who are the introverts?
- Who are the observers?
- Whom do you immediately relate to? Why?
- Whom will you have to work hard to get to know?
- How do the other interns relate to supervisors and staff?

Your observations will give you a sense of the group—the leaders, the followers—and will help you understand where you fit in.

Organize Your Observations

After the first few days, take some notes about what you have observed. Use the following chart as a guide:

My First Impressions

Characteristic	Name	Name	Name	Name
Outgoing				
Quiet				
Friendly to all				
Cliquey				
Willing to share				
Experience with group projects				
What they like to do (example: graphics)				
What they don't like to do (example: budgeting)				
How invested they seem				
Ways you think you can work together				
Other observations				
Overall first impression				

Ask and Learn

Everyone loves to talk about his or her experiences. Ask questions. Get to know the other interns. Learn about their interests, where they grew up, where they went to school, and what they are studying. *Find common ground* and start forming relationships *on the very first day.* These early relationships will help you overcome the inevitable challenges of working under group project deadlines.

When looking for common ground, the 80/20 rule is a good rule to follow: Listen 80 percent and talk 20 percent. It's easy to say. It can be hard to do. But if you listen a lot more and talk a lot less, you will learn more and will be better equipped to ask and answer questions.

Now, Figure Out Where the Opportunities Lie

Think about your first impression of the other interns within the context of achieving your internship goal. What opportunities or roadblocks do you think exist for you to achieve your goal? Fill in the following table.

What I Need to Be Aware of to Achieve My Goal

My Goal	Opportunities	Obstacles	My Ideas for Overcoming Obstacles

Fill in this table, even if you are the only intern. This will help you find your place within the team faster and prepare you for goal-oriented conversations with supervisors.

Be Yourself

You probably hear this all the time: "Just be yourself." It's one of those phrases that can be as annoying as it is true. Other interns may have gone to fancier schools or traveled to faraway places. Don't let those facts be intimidating. Remember:

- *You* got this internship.
- *You* were hired because your personality fits with the culture.

- *You* have a lot to offer
- Be confident and focus on doing good work.

Offer Help

Your goal is to become an integral member of the team, so don't hide in your cubicle. Once a day, ask a member of your team, **"How can I help you today?"**

Asking "How can I help you today?" will define you as a "go-to" person. This question communicates confidence.

Be Solutions Oriented

As your internship progresses, business challenges will be presented to you and your squad. It's easy to complain about a challenge or a tight deadline. Don't. No one cares. Solutions are valuable; complaining is not. When you are overcoming challenges in a group setting, be flexible and open minded.

- ✓ Come to group discussions and brainstorming sessions prepared with a possible solution or an idea.
- ✓ Think of your solution as a starting point to the conversation.
- ✓ Don't dig in and be dogmatic about your idea.
- ✓ Be flexible and let other ideas develop within the group.
- ✓ Do your best to adapt to and integrate the ideas of others to find the best possible solution for the challenge.

As we said earlier, your employer will be watching. Problem solving and adaptability are traits that employers value.

Finally, here are two types of interns that may surprise you:

1. Interns Who Don't Want an Internship

Believe it or not, not everyone will be happy to have an internship. Perhaps their parents or school counselors told them that they were expected to get an internship. Maybe, they would rather be at the beach. Or maybe, they're not really interested in the company or the work.

If you come across this type, don't get sucked into a negative mindset, especially if you're serious about your internship and are using it as a potential route to employment. Instead, figure out their areas of strength and involve them in projects that they'll enjoy and where they will excel. They'll be more likely to work well, hit deadlines, and make everyone's experience easier and more enjoyable.

2. The "Connected" Intern

Some of the interns have landed, just like you, through hard work, networking, and planning. Some others may have a personal or family connection and know a lot about the inner workings of the company, its competition, and the industry. Get to know these people! They will help you quickly understand how the company operates and thinks. Talking to these interns will shorten your learning curve and make you more productive and successful.

Down and Dirty Recap

- Observe and listen.
- Ask questions.
- Be yourself.
- Figure out how you can work with the other interns to achieve your goals.
- Follow the 80/20 rule.

What I Know Now (Notes)

What I Need to Do Next (Notes)

PART 3

Launching Your Career

CHAPTER 9

Exceeding Expectations

Managing Up and Around

What You'll Get From This Chapter

This chapter is about two things that will contribute equally to your success as an intern:

- ✓ Managing yourself with supervisors and staff
- ✓ Hearing and incorporating feedback—good and bad

When you're in school, the expectations are clear: Professors teach, while you question, absorb, and learn. The business world is much more fluid. Employees often collaborate, but sometimes they compete to meet shifting business goals. It's challenging because new competitive ideas appear every day.

Your success will be measured by your ability to:

- Collaborate
- Deliver against deadlines
- Manage your time
- Demonstrate an exceptional work ethic

In other words, your success has moved from a black-and-white metric—your grades—to shades of gray.

What the working world offers is the freedom to have a hand in shaping the environment in which you will excel. Your internship may be the first time you are tasked with identifying challenges on your own, coming up with ideas and solutions, and being fully accountable for your work. To do this well, you'll need to communicate effectively and actively manage your relationships with supervisors, staff, and peers. This is a huge opportunity to set yourself apart.

Be Ready for "What Do You Think?"

We've said all along that employers hire interns to hear their solutions and points of view. So don't be surprised by the question "What do you think?"

This is a hard question to answer because it will be asked in the moment, and you'll have to think on your feet. When the question comes, don't panic. Take a deep breath and take a moment to organize your thoughts. Remember, this is your opinion, but hopefully it's based in fact.

Get prepared by staying up to date with what's happening in your industry and how your company fits into its market. Newsfeeds, Google, and your company's press clippings are all important sources.

But don't only rely on the facts. Be prepared to voice your opinion. It is being valued, and that should make you feel great!

Here is some additional advice for understanding and managing expectations.

Find Out What's (Really) Expected

You'll get a good idea of what's expected during orientation. But what you'll hear during orientation speaks to the overall expectations for the internship program. It doesn't speak to individual expectations for each intern. It is up to you to find out what the expectations are for you and to come up with a plan to deliver. Having identified skill sets and a personal goal for your internship will help you begin conversations with staff and supervisors about how to succeed.

Step 1: Find Out How Interns Are Perceived Within the Company

The first step is to find out how interns are perceived in general within the company. Strike up a conversation with your supervisor or other employees and ask the following five questions:

1. "Have you worked with interns in the past?"
2. "What was the best experience you had with an intern?"
3. "What was the worst experience you had with an intern?"
4. "What is your definition of an ideal intern?"
5. "How can I help you while I'm here?"

The answers will help you understand how staff view and use interns, where potential roadblocks lie, and things you should do and not do to succeed.

Here are three additional tips to help you manage staff expectations:

Understand the Team

When you're hired, you will be told about the reporting structure. Your supervisor will oversee your work, but your supervisor also has his or her own work to complete. Your supervisor may be too busy to monitor your daily activities and workflow. During the first few days, figure out the dynamics of your team by paying attention to the following:

- Who really directs the work in the group?
- Who are the "doers" and who are the "delegators"?
- Who seems most in need of extra help?
- Who is most likely to give you work to do?
- Who is most likely to give you feedback and suggestions for improvement?

With these answers, you can better position yourself as an asset to those who need you most.

Communicate

During your first week, schedule a 15- to 20-minute, one-on-one meeting with your supervisor. Plan a few discussion points. Here are some examples of questions you can use to start the meeting (in the meeting, apply the 80/20 rule):

- "How can I be a great intern?" (Be humble and pay attention to the advice!)
- "What is the best way to communicate with you?"
- "What are my daily or weekly tasks?"
- "What are the timelines?"
- "For collaborative projects, who else is on the team, and what is the best way to contact them?"
- "Is there a format you prefer for reporting updates and asking questions, for example, by having a weekly meeting, by e-mail, or by dropping in?"

Trust me, your supervisor will like that you are being proactive. But the most important result is that *you* will know, from the beginning, what's expected and how to report results and challenges. With a 6- to 10-week internship, spending 2 weeks "figuring out the system" cuts down on your productivity and may ultimately reflect on your performance and final recommendation.

Be Proactive

In the beginning, you'll be getting to know the other interns and staff and figuring out the workload and what the team expects. To deliver on their expectations of you and your expectations of yourself, get organized in the following ways:

- *Put your systems in place.* Your work may require paper as well as electronic files. Make sure you have the supplies you need to get and stay organized. In person, be extra nice to the administrative assistants, receptionists, IT support, and the office manager—they know where all the best stuff is kept and how to quickly fix problems.

- *Keep calm but speak up!* It's reasonable to expect that many employees will want your help. Create timelines and prioritize the work to stay on task. If you're not sure about the priorities, ask! Keep the lines of communication open. Because you are an intern, it is not your responsibility to manage multiple and competing deadlines. If you find yourself in a situation where many have asked for your help and the deadlines overlap, don't get stressed out. Ask for help. Other staff may not be aware of who else you are helping.
- *Learn the bigger picture.* When staff members request your help, ask about the larger goal or business objective of the assignment. Learning the bigger picture allows you to understand where you and your work fit into broader business goals. Asking shows that you are invested and interested in the work. After all, you are there to learn, and having a better understanding of the business helps build your knowledge of the sector and your postinternship resume.

Your worst case here is that they don't have time at that moment but invite you to meet later and answer your questions. This is actually your best case, because you will now have one-on-one meeting time with your supervisor.

Step 2: Move Toward What You Want From the Internship

The other side of the expectation intersection is what you want to get out of the internship. To meet your personal expectations, start with the end in mind.

Ask and answer this question: "What do I want to happen after this internship is over?" Here are some possible answers:

- A job offer.
- A good recommendation.
- An introduction to another department or company.
- I don't know yet.

Even if your answer is "I don't know yet," continuously asking the question is a great place to start. You may or may not be offered—or want—a job at the end of your internship, but going to work every day with the mindset of a job offer will increase your level of focus and professionalism. This guarantees that you do your best work every day. At the very least, this attitude will lead to a good recommendation, which will help you get the right job for you.

So, if you know going in what you want coming out, you will be able to make action plans that will keep you focused and more likely to achieve your goals.

Coming Away With a Positive Recommendation

A good recommendation from your supervisor is an important first step toward a job, either here or somewhere else. Ask yourself, *"What exactly do I want this company to say about me after my internship has ended?"* To begin, look back to what you wrote before the beginning of Part 2 about what you thought you wanted your recommendation to say.

When employers write recommendations, they often use stock phrases to signal potential employers and HR departments about your working style and your capabilities. Here are examples of often-used comments so you can decode your recommendation:

Often-Used Comments in Recommendations

Positive Recommendation Phrases	Needs Improvement Recommendation Phrases
Effective public speaker	Would be an effective presenter with coaching
Works well within a team	Prefers working on assignments alone; project relied on the whole team
Manages time and multiple assignments effectively	Issues with completing tasks at deadline
Got along well with colleagues, interns, and staff	Kept primarily to himself or herself; didn't interact with team
Always willing to pitch in	Completed assignments given; did not seek out additional work

Positive Recommendation Phrases	Needs Improvement Recommendation Phrases
A pleasure to have in the office	Worked the full day as required, but exhibited little curiosity about the work
Incorporated advice and feedback well	Had a set way of working and did not exhibit flexibility

Now that you know what you might read from your employer, plan for what you want to read in your recommendation. Here's how to plan to get the recommendation you want:

1. *Visualize the outcome.* We've talked about this before, but visualization is a powerful tool, and it can be used in a lot of different circumstances. In this case, it helps with goal setting and creating timelines against tasks.

    Visualize the moment you are handed your recommendation. What are the words you want to read? Now that you are in and understand the position, write down *exactly* what you want to see in your recommendation later. Having your ideal recommendation already in writing will help you define the activities, tasks, and behaviors needed to get that recommendation.

2. *Make a plan.* Once you have identified the key points of your recommendation, work on your personal action plan. Align your plan with the goal you've set for yourself. Here is an example: If you want to become a better public speaker, look for opportunities to present your work or take on the role of lead presenter for a group project. Identify this goal with your supervisor early on so he or she can help you succeed.

3. *Set up "advice time."* This is where you can let your winning personality shine through. In your initial one-on-one meeting, you talked with your supervisor or mentor about your goal for the internship. In that meeting, your supervisor or mentor likely talked about ideas to help you achieve your goal within the larger business objectives. Now it's your turn to set up an "advice meeting" midway through your internship.

Use this meeting to check in, ask about your performance, find out if you are meeting expectations, and talk about how this connects with your goal. It's also a good time to ask about the specific activities required to get a great recommendation. Don't be shy. If you don't ask, you don't get. Supervisors and mentors are always happy to help you become successful.

If there is a huge disconnect between your supervisor's expectations and your goal, be open to a discussion about reaching a middle ground that works for everyone. Actively listen to and incorporate what your supervisor is saying into your daily work. Better to do a midcourse reset than to be surprised at the end! And always thank your supervisor or mentor for his or her time!

This Really Happened

Paul loved making films. He couldn't remember a time when he didn't want to make films. When he landed an internship in a top production company, he felt like his dreams were coming true. He would meet top industry producers and work with the latest technology.

He couldn't wait to start.

His first few days were spent meeting people, getting coffee, and ordering lunches. That seemed OK in the beginning, but it quickly became clear that getting coffee and lunch *were* his job and that he wouldn't be offered any hands-on production work. At first, Paul was very upset. He felt misled and taken advantage of by the manager. He asked for more responsibility but was denied.

Paul was faced with a choice: *Quit or try to make the best of the situation.*

It occurred to him that although his responsibilities were limited, he needed to find the opportunity in his situation. Paul realized that he controlled something that the owners, executives, and producers all wanted: caffeine and food! So Paul began using his coffee- and food-delivery responsibilities to ask questions and engage the producers in conversation about their work and industry trends.

During his fourth week, an executive recognized Paul's curiosity and asked him to help out on a film in production. This was exactly what Paul wanted.

At the end of his internship, after delivering countless coffees and lunches, Paul had a long list of high-level contacts, concrete production experience, and an inside view of film production.

Standing Tall While Taking Criticism

If you are an athlete, you've heard "*It's not how you fall down; it's how you get up that matters.*" Your first experience in the business world will not be perfect.

Neither will your second, third, fourth…. You get the point. There will be bumps in the road, and at some point, something about your work or your effort will be criticized.

When you receive constructive criticism, you'll probably be caught off guard. Your first reaction may be to object to what you are hearing. Don't.

Part of being considered as a potential employee will be based on how you deal with constructive criticism and adversity in the moment. You will be judged on "how you get up." Practice your responses for this conversation. Here are some examples:

1. "Thank you for taking the time to analyze my performance. I want to improve [X]. Do you have some time to work on putting together an action plan with me?"

   This response shows your ability to be adaptable and respond quickly and unemotionally in real time.

2. "Thank you for your feedback. I would like to think about what you said and meet again tomorrow. Does that work for you?"

   This is a good response when you're shocked, angry, or believing that the feedback is unjustified.

   Waiting a day will take the bite out of your response and give you time to:
   - Be open to listening to *why* there is criticism.
   - Build a *factual* case for why you believe your actions were appropriate.
   - Tone down your emotions.

   Supervisors aren't always right, but they will expect a professional conversation.

3. "Wow, I really thought I was headed down the right road. Thanks for being honest. I could really use your advice for getting back on track."

   Use this response if you are ready to have a productive, unemotional conversation right away. This is especially useful when you are working on a tight deadline and don't have the luxury of waiting a day to respond. Do your best to smile and thank your supervisor for spending time thinking about this issue. This accomplishes two things:
   1. It gives you a few seconds to prepare your reply.
   2. It tells the person delivering the news that you can graciously accept constructive feedback and even criticism.

How you respond is yet another opportunity for creating a positive impression.

There Is No Intern Emoji for a Reason

What you do after a conversation that includes constructive feedback really matters. This is not a social media opportunity! If a supervisor criticizes you or your work and you are hurt or angry, do not go back to your desk and complain on Facebook, over text, or out loud to other interns. If you are upset, go outside, walk around the block, go to the cafeteria, or even hang out in the restroom for a few minutes and calm down. You'll be judged by your actions during these times, and in an office with an open floor plan, your activities and conversations are in plain view of staff and the other interns.

Learning how to act in an environment designed for doing, not learning, is a big adjustment. Some companies are more equipped than others for teaching interns. Regardless, having a goal and an action plan of your own will help guide you to succeed and move toward the outcome and recommendation you want from your internship experience.

Down and Dirty Recap

- Visualize the recommendation you want.
- Create action plans.
- Ask for advice from supervisors.
- "Read" the environment.
- Accept constructive criticism and feedback graciously.
- Thank staff for their time and their help.
- Prepare for "What do you think?"

What I Know Now (Notes)

What I Need to Do Next (Notes)

CHAPTER 10

Interns in the Wild

What You'll Get From This Chapter

This chapter prepares you to excel every day in a new environment. We'll focus on how you'll want to handle yourself throughout the intern project and other important office activities.

In this new world, you'll be judged by your *ability to adapt* to:

- ✓ Subject matter that's new
- ✓ Collaborators who are not of your choosing
- ✓ Supervisors who have little interest in becoming friends (not all, but some)
- ✓ Unexpected changes in deadlines and work priorities
- ✓ The unpredictable schedules of others

Effectively navigating all of this, and more, is part of the last impression you'll leave with the organization. Even if you plan on never coming back to the company, assume that one day someone will call the company for information about your performance as an intern. You'll want that call to be positive!

Managing Yourself During the Intern Project

Many companies have intern programs structured around a project. The project is designed for the employer to observe how you work and learn your perspective on a business goal or challenge. If your particular program does not involve a project, keep reading. What follows will help you navigate the environment and successfully manage yourself and your workload.

Whether there's a project or not, start to think of everything you do as a hiring test. If your internship involves a project, approach it like a long, long interview. Within a controlled environment, the project allows employers to watch how interns:

- Incorporate *problem-solving* skills and work *collaboratively*
- Work toward solving business challenges
- *Adapt* to change
- Demonstrate *leadership* and *humility*
- Communicate—especially under pressure

Sounds familiar? It's many of the Big Six, and it's a great chance to stand out and show what you can do!

What follows is an example of how an intern project is structured.

The Assignment

- Research, create, and present to senior leadership a 12-month marketing plan for a prospective or existing client.

The Structure

- Interns are expected to work together and utilize full-time staff and company resources to achieve objectives.
- A senior executive acts as an advisor.
- Final presentations to the intern leadership team will take place on [date].

Development of a marketing plan is a good example of a project, as every company, regardless of its product, must position its value to present and future customers. And today's young interns may very well be tomorrow's customers.

If your intern project is well researched and presented, there is a small chance that it might be shared with a broader internal group or an outside client. If that happens, ask to attend that meeting. After all, you were part of the work. It's an opportunity to see how the work is used to create a well-constructed pitch. If the work is being used in an external client meeting and you can attend, you will see how the company talks about and presents itself to the outside world.

Go Team!

A successful project comes from good collaboration. Here are five tips to help you both collaborate and stand out as you work on the intern project.

1. *Get clarity.* As soon as the project is assigned, make sure that the details and timelines for completion of each phase are clear. If something hasn't been fully explained, ask for an explanation right away. This will help avoid the dreadful "Oh, we didn't know" that leads to last-minute, flat-out panic. If you don't know what or how to ask, try asking these questions:

    "What has worked well with similar projects?"

    "What haven't we asked that will help us get started?"

2. *Avoid infighting.* Good collaboration means acting as both a leader and a humble worker. If an Alpha intern is grabbing control of the project, *speak up!* Keep the goal you set for your internship way back in Chapter 3 in mind. Deciding who leads different pieces of the project will move things forward *and* allow everyone the opportunity to accomplish personal goals. If others in your group have similar goals, decide who owns which piece so everyone can highlight their strengths.

    If you are getting pushback about leading a piece of the project, work to bring the other interns around to your point of view. Talk about the value you bring and how your work will make everyone be more successful. If this fails and you are committed to owning an aspect of the project, ask your supervisor or a trusted employee for advice. Be prepared to make the *business case*. Don't complain. Explain your experience and be clear about *why* you should lead that section. Listen to and follow your supervisor's advice. Tread lightly because, as the first exposure to the working world, the other interns are the foundation of your professional network. If you get rejected, roll with it. Consider it a test of your flexibility and your ability to collaborate.

3. *Take notes.* Decide on a note-taker for every meeting to keep track of conversations and track progress to goals. To keep everyone invested, rotate this task equally among all interns. A written record creates accountability and allows any intern to confidently answer any question from staff, at any time.

4. *Work backward.* Create a timeline with benchmarks to measure progress. Be *aggressively optimistic* in your benchmark planning. This will work in your favor when deadlines and priorities change—as they often do. Last-minute adjustments in workflow will allow you to demonstrate your ability to adapt.

5. *Let ideas flow.* Build in time to brainstorm and build out ideas—not just at the beginning of the work, but throughout the process. Coming up with ideas as a group creates mutual ownership and solidifies your team.

   Groups that work as a team do a better job at the final presentation. Here is how to set up a productive brainstorming session:

   - Decide on the *one thing* the group will work on in the session.
   - To help the group stay on task, write the task on a flipchart or whiteboard.
   - Ask for a volunteer to write down the ideas from the session.
   - Set a time limit and assign a timekeeper for each phase of the session.
   - Create action items for each new idea that's worth pursuing.
   - Ask for volunteers to work on specific action items.
   - Before ending any team meeting, take time for "final comments." Doing so ensures that no one's ideas or thoughts have been overlooked.
   - Outline next steps and the owner of the activity.

   Getting input from everyone is critical because *people support what they create.* Coming up with new ideas requires brainpower and a relaxed environment. Food helps. Ask your supervisor if there is a budget for food to fuel your brainstorming sessions. Your supervisor will see the team as taking the project seriously, and you'll all get a free meal. If three pizzas generate one idea, it's a great deal for everyone.

6. *It's showtime!* As a last step, the intern group will present the results of its project to the staff. Executives are busy people, and most will tell you they spend too much time in meetings. So, respect their time and yours by practicing your presentation in advance!

Decide in advance who will say what, when, and why. This is called putting together a "run of show" (ROS). Lay out an ROS to ensure that each presenter gets a fair turn in front of the room and that you do not exceed your time limit. Use the following schedule to set up your ROS.

Run of Show Schedule

Subject: Intern Project [X]
Timeframe: 45 minutes including Q&A
Date: [XX]

Topic	Speaker	Duration	Supporting Info/AV	Info/AV Tech Person
Introduction	Sue	10:00–10:05	Title slide	N/A
Project objectives	Bob	10:05–10:10	Video/PowerPoint slide 1	Sue
Research	Alicia	10:10–10:20	PowerPoint slides 2–4	Sue
Recommendations	Doug	10:20–10:30	PowerPoint slides 5–6	Sue
Q&A	All	10:30–10:45	Questions/Thank you slide	Sue

With an ROS, your group will stand out, sound professional, and end on time—all factors that executives appreciate. If possible, your practice sessions should take place in the same space and use the same tech you'll use for your final presentation.

Now that you've mastered the intern project, let's move on to everyone's favorite topic: meetings.

How to Be Awesome in Meetings

Depending on the agenda, you may have other people outside of your department in a meeting. This is yet another opportunity to make a positive impression. Staff will notice how you handle yourself. Being well thought of increases the likelihood you'll be brought in on interesting projects with people from different departments. In the long term, this expands your professional network. In the short term, the impression you leave in meetings is a factor your supervisor will consider when writing your recommendation. In both cases, leaving a positive impression with a roomful of people can help you later in your career or a job search.

Here are some dos and don'ts for the types of meetings you're likely to encounter. The don'ts may seem obvious or silly, but they're on the list because they happened to people just like you. Learn from the mistakes of others—it's far less painful!

Scenario	Do	Don't	Why
Meetings with staff (Your department)	• Be on time • Bring a pen and paper • Take notes • Ask a smart question	• Be late • Be on your phone	You are judged based on the interest you show in the work and the quality of your questions Phones are distracting
"All Hands" meetings (Many attendees, usually held in a large conference room)	• Arrive early • Sit in the back or along a wall • Take notes • Listen for information that will help in the intern project • Write down questions for your supervisor	• Sit at the conference table, even if chairs are available. These are for senior managers who may be running late. Contribute, until you understand how the meeting works or until you are asked	These are big meetings designed to share information and report progress. Taking notes signals that you are interested in the company's activities

Scenario	Do	Don't	Why
Group lunch with staff	• Go even if you are swamped	• Complain about your workload	Everyone you meet is a networking opportunity or even a potential employer
Happy Hour with staff	• Go even if you aren't 21. It's a great chance to connect with staff	• Have more than one drink—assuming you are 21—regardless of how much the staff is drinking	Every interaction with staff is an interview. Getting buzzed with staff may be fun in the moment but will not reflect well on you later
When your supervisor occasionally asks you to run out and get coffee or lunch	• Say yes and deliver in a timely manner	• Cop an attitude	Remember, as an intern, you are there to help. Use your delivery as an opportunity to ask questions

This Really Happened

At a large All Hands meeting, Stevie, the intern, arrived early and took an empty seat at the conference table. No one told her that the chairman usually sat in that chair.

When the chairman and COO arrived, they "asked" Stevie to stand up and move to the back of the room. Fifty people watched Stevie's walk of shame. This is an avoidable embarrassment! Ask your supervisor about the seating protocol for large meetings. When in doubt, choose the back of the room.

Dealing With the Unpredictable

Business can be messy. Unexpected stuff happens all the time. Expect the unexpected. How you react in the moment will be an important part of your end-of-internship evaluation.

Here are some scenarios that have happened to others and some ideas for how to react well in the moment.

Top Five "What Do I Do If" Questions You May Face

1. *"What do I do if my supervisor cancels our meetings and is always too busy to meet with me?"*

Action Steps

- Don't complain.
- Acknowledge in person or by e-mail that you understand it's a busy time and that it's difficult to keep meetings on the schedule.
- Offer alternative ways to communicate. For example, suggest a breakfast meeting, an informal lunch in the break room, or a catch-up by phone or video chat.
- Then, follow up with an e-mail to your supervisor along the lines of the following:

  Subject line: [Your name] *Progress Report*

  Dear [supervisor],

  I understand it's a busy time and that it's been difficult for us to meet in person. This e-mail provides an update on my active projects, the outstanding issues, and the expected completion dates.

  [Insert your chart here]

  I look forward to your feedback.

  Please let me know if there is a convenient time to discuss the projects further.

  Thank you. Sincerely, [Your name]

- When you do get a meeting, have your questions and issues ready!
- You can also ask other staff members for advice on the best way to communicate with the supervisors.

2. *"What do I do if there isn't enough work to do?"*

Action Steps

- Don't complain.
- Ask your supervisor if there are any long-term projects that you could research.
- Offer to assist in another department.
- Make up a project. For example, offer an analysis of how people your age relate to the company's product or service.
- Read trade publications to become more informed about the industry and develop questions for your supervisor and staff.

3. *"What do I do if my day is spent running mindless errands for senior executives?"*

Action Steps

- It's a less-than-perfect scenario, but don't complain.
- Turn errand running into an opportunity. Every errand either begins or ends with an interaction with an executive. Use these opportunities to network. (See Paul's story in Chapter 9.)
- When you return from an errand, ask the executive if he or she has a moment for *one* question. Prepare your question in advance. For example:

  Hi. Here is your latte. Do you have a moment for one quick question? I was reading in [XX: newspaper, trade publication, etc.] *about* [XX] *and was wondering how does that affect this company and your role?*

- If the errand begins and ends with the senior executive's assistant, try to become friends. Over time, these gatekeepers can help you. Most of the time you can make this scenario positive.
  - Continue to ask your boss for "real" responsibilities. It's possible that your boss is not aware that you're running errands all day.

- ○ If other responsibilities don't materialize, think about asking if you would be better utilized in another department.
- ○ If you've exhausted all the options, you may be faced with a decision to stay or to pursue another outside opportunity.

4. *"What do I do if I don't like the other interns to the point where we can't collaborate?"*

Action Steps

- Don't complain.
- Try to find common ground with at least one other intern.
- Focus on the intern project and what you have promised to deliver.
- Get to know the people in other departments; perhaps your skills could be better used in another department.

5. *"What do I do if I love the company, but not the department?"*

Action Steps

- Don't complain.
- Give your internship some time. You may need to grow into the position.
- Find tasks that are better suited to your skills.
- Internships are about learning. Take away as much as you can from the opportunity.

    After a trial period, you may find that where you've been placed doesn't fit with your skills and/or interests.

If this happens, be honest. Your supervisor may be willing to help you find a better fit in another department.

Down and Dirty Recap

- Understand every aspect of the intern project.
- Brainstorm often.
- Learn the etiquette for meetings and outings.
- Be ready to adapt to the unexpected.
- If the internship isn't what you expected, don't complain. Act.

What I Know Now (Notes)

What I Need to Do Next (Notes)

CHAPTER 11

Saying Goodbye to Your Internship and Hello to the Working World

What You'll Get From This Chapter

We'll set you up to leave well, to be remembered in a good way, and if you choose, to ask for a full-time job.

You already know that a positive first impression is critical to your future.

But have you ever thought about the last impression you leave? How you leave a job is just as important as how you start. It's possible that your last impression as an intern could serve as your first impression as an employee.

Simply put, your performance and attitude during the last weeks of your internship are what colleagues or referral sources will remember most about you. This assumes that you've not had any major missteps along the way.

The people with whom you've intersected in these last weeks are now part of your professional network and will be important resources during your job search. The good news is that with a little extra work, you *can* do a lot to control what will be said about you in a reference call.

Imagine that, at some point in the future, an HR screener calls the office where you've interned to ask for a reference. Most companies will confirm your dates of employment. After that, they don't *have* to say anything, positive or negative.

But if you've performed well *and* leave well, this is how the staff might **talk about you after you're gone:**

- "I liked her from the start. She went above and beyond and came through on the project."
- "He was just as enthusiastic about the job on his last day as he was on his first."
- "She was very helpful and managed her time really well. I'm going to miss working with her."

In a reference check, these comments mean "Take a close look at this candidate. This candidate is an asset."

Alternatively, this is **how you don't want the staff to talk about you after you're gone:**

- "Well, she does good work, but she has a lot to learn about collaboration."
- "In meetings or presentations, she loves the spotlight—maybe a bit too much."
- "He has a bit to learn about follow-up."

When comments like these find their way into a reference check, the message is either "Look closely before hiring" or "Don't hire!"

Checklist: "Will My Last Impression Be Positive?"

Answer yes or no to the following questions. Be honest!

- "Did I work with many different people in the company?"
- "Was I helpful?"
- "Did I ask staff for advice and leverage their experience to help solve a challenge?"
- "Did I thank those who helped me—*in the moment?*"

- "Did I follow up regularly?"
- "Did I not complain when things did not go my way?"
- "Did I graciously take on work?"
- "Did I show interest in the company and its challenges?"
- "Did I lead problem-solving efforts on my intern team?"
- "Did I advance the mission and interests of the firm?"

How did you answer these questions? If you feel you could do better, then use these last few weeks to turn "No" answers to "Yes."

The Last Two Weeks: Top 10 Things to Do

The last weeks of an internship often involve a lot of "housekeeping" tasks and a lot of goodbyes. But there are some simple and fun things to do that will go far toward leaving a great last impression.

Here are the 10 topics that we will cover in this section:

1. Feedback on Your Work
2. Asking for Constructive Criticism
3. Telling the Story of Your Experience
4. Asking for a Written Recommendation
5. Your Last Visual Impression
6. Thank You Notes
7. Gifts
8. The Exit Interview
9. How to Ask for a Job
10. Staying in Touch

1. Feedback on Your Work

If your supervisor does not bring this up, be sure to ask for a "short meeting to hear feedback on my work." You have five important questions. The answers will indicate the kind of reference or recommendation you'll get from this individual. During your job search, the answers to these questions will factor into whom you choose to offer as references. Listen carefully. Take notes.

1. "What did I do well?"
2. "Where can I improve?"
3. "How was my performance perceived within the company?"
4. *For students:* "As I go back to school, what kinds of classes should I be thinking about if I want to work in [XX]?"
5. *For all:* "What additional training would help me prepare for a career in [X]?"

2. Asking for Constructive Feedback

When you ask for feedback, also ask for constructive criticism. Both help you shape your working habits and routines in the future.

If the critical feedback is minimal, ask for any additional thoughts or advice.

> **Example:** "Completing a project against a floating deadline is something new for me. Is there any advice you can offer from your experience so I can get better at this?"
>
> If, however, the criticism is substantial, listen carefully but don't argue about individual points. It's too late to do much about it. Telling a supervisor or HR that "you're wrong, and don't get it" is neither constructive nor a useful part of the last impression you leave at the company. Absolutely advocate for yourself, but don't argue. Arguing without evidence doesn't benefit you or your last impression.

A Story: Problem, Solution, and Outcome in 59 Words

> An hour before we were scheduled to present the Big Idea we'd developed for the internship project, the entire printer network crashed. We needed 30 copies. We found a Staples, spoke to the manager, and e-mailed the presentation to the store, got an Uber,

picked it up, and got back to the office with 10 minutes to spare. It was terrifying—and fun!

3. Telling the Story of Your Experience

People forget details and facts, but they rarely forget a good story.

Go into the meeting prepared to tell a short, memorable story involving a learning experience. You can talk about overcoming a challenge, meeting a deadline, working with others, or something funny that bonded the team together. Here are guidelines for constructing a story for this meeting, and an example:

- *Make it short.* Your goal is to make the story memorable and repeatable.
- *Identify a challenge.* Every story needs a villain! This can be a tight deadline, a resource that wasn't available, or some other challenge that you overcame or problem that you solved.
- *Communicate an outcome.* An outcome is the result of your work.

4. Asking for a Written Recommendation

Don't be shy! You've done the work. You've had a great experience. You've left a great impression. Now it's time to get it on paper. When looking for candidates, employers seek out and value recommendations from professional peers. That means that your supervisor will likely be willing to write you a recommendation. If you're in person, *ask for a recommendation before you leave the building for the last time.* It should contain:

- An overall assessment of your performance
- A picture of your working style
- A summary of your strengths and areas for improvement

Ask that the recommendation be sent to you electronically so that you can easily forward it to prospective employers. Also, ask if your supervisor would be willing to write a recommendation to post on your LinkedIn profile. LinkedIn recommendations make you a stronger candidate. Then, add your internship experience to your profile, sign up for LinkedIn's job alerts, and let the search engines do their job. Even if you've received some negative feedback, don't despair. After all, this is your first job, and the expectation is not perfection. Again, what employers look for are *adaptability, a helpful nature, a collaborative spirit,* and *a teachable attitude.* In a nondefensive way, you can advocate for yourself and highlight your performance.

5. Your Last Visual Impression

As we've talked about earlier, impressions and looks matter. Pay extra attention to how you dress and how you look during your last week. Keep showing up early. You want to be perceived as enthusiastic from beginning to end.

In person: Even if your office has Casual Friday, be sure to dress in "office attire" on your last Friday. In a world where people remember what they see, avoid a last impression that is too casual. What staff will remember is the visual impression, not that it was Casual Friday. "Dressing the part" subconsciously triggers a more professional impression. Use this to your advantage.

6. Thank You Notes

Handwritten is preferred, remembered, and a very easy way to set yourself apart from other interns. Guidelines include the following:

- Use high-quality stationery.
- Don't use cute gimmicks or Emojis on the front.
- Make a list in advance of who is to receive a note, so you don't leave anyone out by accident. Recipients should include the following:
  - Everyone you worked with directly.
  - HR.

- ○ Contacts you made along the way.
- ○ People who could help you in the future.
- Where appropriate, begin with "Thank you" for their advice, guidance, and support.
- If possible, include a story.
- Close with a promise to stay in touch, and then *do* stay in touch.

It takes a bit longer to write a personal note, but it pays off every time.

This Really Happened

Three years after his internship, Liam ran into his internship supervisor on the street. The supervisor told him that she had kept his handwritten note and that it had become her standard for all thank you notes.

If using snail mail: Mail the notes during the last week of your internship so that they arrive early the next week.

7. Gifts

For the staff members who helped you and your team throughout the internship, it's polite to acknowledge them with a small group gift. Although not required, a gift that connects to something that happened during the internship, to the intern project, or to a group outing is always fun.

When thinking about a gift, consider something that can be used in the office. This accomplishes three things:

1. The gift is functional.
2. The gift is a constant reminder of you and your group.
3. The gift is small enough to fit on a shelf or desk.

The gift becomes one more thing to support your positive last impression.

8. *The Exit Interview or Survey*

Depending on the formality of your internship program, you may have an exit interview or asked to fill out a survey. Exit interviews help the program managers improve the internship program. Your input matters.

The exit interview is not the time to rehash gripes about other interns or staff. The interviewer is looking for actionable ways to improve future programs. Whether you want to work at this company or somewhere else, it's important to plan what you say and how you say it. Here are some guidelines for the conversation.

Begin on a positive note. Lay out what you think worked well, and *why*.

Be prepared to discuss the following:

- What you liked
- What you learned
- What can improve
- The biggest challenge
- The biggest surprise
- Your most important takeaways from the internship

You'll likely be asked for your feedback about the company culture. Creating and maintaining a positive culture where employees are valued, satisfied, and productive is a daily HR conversation.

Your suggestions should connect with a work goal and/or improved productivity. ***If you have a criticism about the program, be prepared to offer a solution.*** Here are some guidelines for solution-focused conversations:

- Be constructive, not critical.
- Have one solution for every criticism.
- Practice delivery of your solutions.
- Be humble. For example, you might say, "What ***may have*** worked better for our particular group was...."

Practice what you want to say. Without advance preparation, it's too easy to slip into complaining mode. Your goal is to be remembered as being positive and action oriented.

Fit

Not all experiences in your working life will be great. If the internship was not what you expected, and there was no action on the part of the company to adjust, it's possible that this experience was simply a bad fit. Focus on what you learned and plan your conversation to include suggestions for the future. Be yourself, but don't be too emotional during the conversation.

This Really Happened

As a rising sophomore in college, Katy loved public relations and took an internship in New York City with a small, scrappy, women-owned firm. The principals told her that she would be the "right hand" and would "be involved every day." What they didn't tell her was that the "right hand" would be wearing a rubber glove and she'd be cleaning and reorganizing the office shelves and supply closets. She tried everything to involve herself in other areas with no success. The internship was just a bad fit.

But the experience was *not* without value. A year later, while interviewing for her next intern position, Katy told the story of her experience at the PR firm. She used the story to explain her goal for the new position. This time around, she was much more specific with questions about roles and responsibilities. She contacted former interns to hear about their experience. As a result, Katy landed a great job with a company that valued her experience, not her ability to clean!

How to Ask for a Job

You've worked hard, been helpful, and enjoyed your internship. Now you'd like to be part of the permanent staff.

If you've not been approached with a job offer, don't let your last week pass by without speaking up. Ask your supervisor for a short meeting and let your supervisor know that you'd like to talk about future employment. This gives your supervisor time to plan how to help you, to speak with

Human Resources, and to speak with other departments to learn about their hiring needs.

Your "asking for a job" mantra is simple:

Be clear.
Be concise.
Be quick.
Be quiet.
Listen.

What to Say and Do in the "Asking for a Job" Meeting

Begin by thanking your supervisor for taking the time to meet. Then do the following:

- Explain that you'd like to be considered for full-time employment.
- State your value proposition (see later).
- Ask for advice about opportunities, the likelihood you will be hired, and how best to proceed. Your supervisor may recommend talking to a department head or to Human Resources.
- Ask what else you can do.
- Thank the person for his or her time.
- Follow up with a thank you note or e-mail.

Your Value Proposition

You now have an inside view of how a company operates. It's a big advantage. Your value will, in part, be based on *the latest skills you've developed and how you can help the company succeed.* When you are explaining your internship experience to new potential employers, organize your narrative in much the same way you organized your resume summary. Be sure to explain the following:

- Who you are
- What you do
- How you'd benefit the company

Be clear. Be concise. Be confident. Here's an example of how to explain your value to an employer:

> My internship was a great experience. As a math major, I used my math skills every day. I would like to talk about opportunities to use my skills in business development or on your analytics team. By the time I graduate, I will have taken five more courses in advanced mathematics which I believe will be an asset to the company.

It's important that your value proposition be brief so people can remember and repeat it accurately. Be specific about what you offer and, if possible, where you would like to apply your skills. Your goal is for the conversation between your exit interviewer and Human Resources to sound like this:

> Alycia was an intern this summer with great *math skills*. She would be a real asset to the company. Are there any open positions *in business development or analytics*?

If you are not sure where you fit in, you can still talk about your value. Go back to the Big Six—the qualities that employers value. Build your value proposition around one or more of these elements:

- Teach-ability
- Adaptability
- Collaboration
- Problem solving
- Humility
- Leadership (which is not mutually exclusive with humility)

Then, ask for advice about where these qualities will fit best within the company. Have specific examples to support your case. Once you have your value proposition, practice it so it will be concise and clear in the meeting.

After You Make Your Request, Stop Talking and Listen

After asking about hiring opportunities, stop talking and listen, and be ready for questions. The conversation may involve open positions, introductions to different departments, or other skills you should consider learning or developing before being considered as a candidate.

Staying in Touch

Congratulations! You have completed your internship and exit interview. Good work. Now you deserve a break before you head back to school or focus on a job search.

As you move on to your next phase, keep in touch with the staff and the other interns. Let the staff know what you've been doing—but don't be a pest! If your internship ends in August and you graduate the following May, plan on checking in two or three times during the school year on e-mail or through LinkedIn. When you do, have something relevant to share. Here are some ideas:

- Include how you're applying what you learned during your internship in school or in your job search.
- Reiterate your timeline for graduation and full-time employment. "I will be graduating in May and would like to contact you again in [X] to talk about any opportunities at the company."
- Ask if you can be of any help to them.

Easy ways to stay in touch are these:

- Send a holiday card with a personal note.
- Ask for a half hour "coffee date" to catch up. It's a nice gesture. Offer to pay.
- Consider this your first business expense.
- Forward an interesting article with a short note.

When you are ready to begin your job hunt in earnest, reconnect with your contacts or Human Resources. If the company isn't currently hiring, you can ask for introductions to colleagues. Be sure to pay it forward by thanking your contact with a coffee or lunch date.

Working your professional network begins as an intern and never really stops.

Down and Dirty Recap

- Plan for your last impression.
- Write a value proposition.
- Ask for feedback—both positive and negative.
- Offer solutions with the feedback you give.
- Practice your stories.
- Ask for a recommendation or a job.
- Listen more; talk less.
- Send thank you notes.

What I Know Now (Notes)

What I Need to Do Next (Notes)

Final Words

Your internship has been quite a ride. You've learned a lot and picked up valuable, real-world experience.

Work, like everything else in life, is a journey. Most likely, you'll make some good decisions along the way, and some that are less than good.

You are coming into the workforce at a time of unlimited opportunity:

Learn every day.
Be yourself.
Be memorable.
Be adaptable.
Listen closely.
Let others help you.
Love what you do.

This is your life. Make it what you want.
Happy Adulting!

About the Author

Marti Fischer is a New York City-based executive coach, blogger, and speaker, specializing in taking the "scary" out of career transitions and transforming managers into leaders. She graduated from Sarah Lawrence College, is certified in basic mediation, and has two children who were successful interns and are now fully employed.

Index

Concise and Applied Business Books

The Collection listed above is one of 30 business subject collections that Business Expert Press has grown to make BEP a premiere publisher of print and digital books. Our concise and applied books are for…

- Professionals and Practitioners
- Faculty who adopt our books for courses
- Librarians who know that BEP's Digital Libraries are a unique way to offer students ebooks to download, not restricted with any digital rights management
- Executive Training Course Leaders
- Business Seminar Organizers

Business Expert Press books are for anyone who needs to dig deeper on business ideas, goals, and solutions to everyday problems. Whether one print book, one ebook, or buying a digital library of 110 ebooks, we remain the affordable and smart way to be business smart. For more information, please visit www.businessexpertpress.com, or contact sales@businessexpertpress.com.

Printed in the USA
CPSIA information can be obtained
at www.ICGtesting.com
LVHW051630301124
797961LV00002B/255